White Man Sleeps

Creative Insights

White Man Sleeps
Creative Insights

Edited by
Sanjoy Roy

DANCE BOOKS
Cecil Court London

Cover Photograph: Lauren Potter in *White Man Sleeps*
                     Photograph by David Buckland

Editorial Co-ordinator: Kirsty Lloyd

Editor: Sanjoy Roy

Contributors: Siobhan Davies
                     Paul Douglas
                     Natalie Gordon
                     Simon Gough
                     Sanjoy Roy
                     Sarah Whatley

Education Advisor: Natalie Gordon

Photographs: David Buckland
                     Hugo Glendinning
                     Sean Hudson

Design: Sanjoy Roy

Published in 1999 by
Dance Books Ltd
15 Cecil Court
London WC2N 4EZ

Copyright © Siobhan Davies Dance Company 1999

ISBN 1 85273 072 2

A CIP catalogue record for this book
is available from the British Library

Printed in Great Britain by
H. Charlesworth & Co. Ltd, Huddersfield

Contents

Appendices

Acknowledgements

Many people have been involved in the production of *White Man Sleeps: Creative Insights*. Thanks go first to David Leonard, the publisher, for his belief in the project. My thanks also to the contributors, who willingly gave much of their time to the book. Sarah Whatley wrote much of the text, and her in-depth knowledge of both *White Man Sleeps* and Siobhan Davies's work was invaluable. Natalie Gordon was the educational advisor, and also created the Labanotation examples. Paul Douglas danced in the original piece, and his contribution provides a unique insider's perspective on the dance. Simon Gough interviewed Siobhan Davies, and provided the opening section of the book.

I am grateful also to the creators of the dance for agreeing to be interviewed, and who all came up with valuable words, information and ideas: Siobhan Davies herself, ever articulate, whose input was vital; Kevin Volans, the composer; David Buckland, the designer; and Peter Mumford, the lighting designer and director of the film.

David Buckland and Hugo Glendinning kindly granted permission to reproduce their photographs, while the Scottish Theatre Archives at Glasgow University Library allowed us to use the photographs by Sean Hudson. I am also grateful to Chester Music for permission to reproduce excerpts of the music score, to Sasha Keir for the use of her costume sketch, and to Kathrine Sorley Walker, John Percival, Stephanie Jordan, Judith Mackrell, Louise Levene and Debra Craine for allowing us to print of excerpts of their reviews.

Finally, I wish to acknowledge the support and guidance of Siobhan Davies Dance Company throughout the whole undertaking. I am indebted in particular to Simon Gough, the marketing manager, and most of all to Kirsty Lloyd, the company administrator, who managed the whole the project, and steered it through from inception to completion.

Sanjoy Roy
September 1999

Contributors

Paul Douglas

After dancing with London Contemporary Dance Theatre, Paul Douglas was a founding member of the Siobhan Davies Dance Company in 1988, and founded his own company Small Bones in 1993. He teaches extensively in the UK and abroad. He is also an Aikido practitioner, and is currently the Head Master of Tetsushinkan Budojo at Moving East.

Natalie Gordon

After graduating from Roehampton Institute London, Natalie Gordon trained as a professional notator at the Labanotation Institute. Since then she has taught widely as a freelance A-level teacher in schools and colleges, and is currently also administrator for Retina Dance Company.

Sanjoy Roy

Sanjoy Roy is an editor, writer and designer. He co-edits and designs the quarterly magazine *Dance Now*, for which he also writes. He has edited and designed numerous publications for Dance Books Ltd, as well as designing video covers for Dance Videos. He is currently on the editorial board for ADiTi, and has also written programme notes for Siobhan Davies Dance Company, and Shobana Jeyasingh Dance Company.

Sarah Whatley

Sarah Whatley is Head of Performing Arts at Coventry University and has responsibility for a range of practice-based courses in performing arts. She designed the BA (Hons) Dance and Professional Practice, and co-ordinated Coventry's New Dance Festival for ten years, until 1998. Her recent performing work includes touring four solo dances, two in collaboration with composers. She is also a graduate researcher at Roehampton Institute London, working towards her PhD investigating the movement vocabulary of Siobhan Davies.

Using This Book

Siobhan Davies began her professional choreographic career in 1972, and has since become one of Britain's most highly acclaimed contemporary choreographers. A founding member of London Contemporary Dance Theatre, she became resident choreographer for that company, and went on to found Second Stride in the early 1980s (with Richard Alston and Ian Spink), later also becoming associate choreographer for Rambert Dance Company. In 1988 she formed Siobhan Davies Dance Company, whose opening programme featured two major works: *Wyoming* and *White Man Sleeps*. This book is an in-depth guide to the creation and choreography of *White Man Sleeps*, based on the film version directed by Peter Mumford, available on video.

In designing the book, we considered one fundamental question: how do we watch a dance? The simple answer is: from start to finish. But while we do this, all sorts of other connections are being made. Our minds skip backwards to an image we've seen before; or we anticipate what is to come next. A memory is triggered, a moment suspended; a longing is ignited, or a tension eased. We may focus on a particular dancer or a grouping; or perhaps our eyes rake across the spaces between them. As we watch and feel the movement – or stillness – our ears are simultaneously hear sounds – or silence. We see the shifting casts of light and shade, register the scenes and setting, the colour and contour of costumes. And all the while, our own experiences, knowledge and personal background are brought to bear on the dance: how much do we recognise about this type of dance? Is it familiar or strange? Who is the choreographer, who are these dancers? And if the dance engages us, it tugs at our imaginations and, magically, insinuates itself into our very bodies.

White Man Sleeps, choreographed by Siobhan Davies in 1988, is a piece that does all these things. While watching the dance a myriad elements come into play. Accordingly, this book is designed to operate on several levels, to suggest many layers and interconnections. Like the work itself, it is divided into five parts, which can be read in sequence, though each also stands on its own. Weaving through these parts, certain ideas recur like motifs, appearing in different contexts, seen from different angles.

Alongside this main text are images, music notation and tables, as well as many annotations:

▶ Those marked with a triangle link backwards or forwards to other parts of the text.

→ Those marked with an arrow refer to other sources, listed in the bibliography.

● Notes marked with a circle refer to a series of suggested tasks, both practical and theoretical, which are given at the end of each chapter.

Supplementing the main text, these annotations suggest some of the different routes and points of entry that can guide us into engaging with the piece.

White Man Sleeps is currently on the A-level syllabus, and the book is also designed as a resource for teachers and students, though we hope that it will also have a broader value than the study of this one particular piece. The tasks given at the end of each section are suggestions for educational use, and include both written and practical exercises, and topics for discussion. In Part 3, there are also a series of Labanotation examples, with exercises, for those studying notation. All these tasks are designed as stimulus and suggestion, and do not necessarily indicate particular questions on examination papers.

This descriptions of *White Man Sleeps* in this book are based on the film version of the work, and this guide is offered as a companion to the video. Like the film, the book is a collaborative venture, and so offers a variety of angles and perspectives on the dance. Like the film too, it can be followed from beginning to end – if you wish. Alternatively you can forward, rewind, pause, or jump cut between long perspective and close focus as the inclination takes you. Above all, the book, like the film – and, ultimately, *White Man Sleeps* itself – is an invitation for creative exploration.

Part 1
Openings

**Siobhan Davies in conversation
with Simon Gough**

*Siobhan Davies discusses the place
of White Man Sleeps in the growth
of her choreography*

A Dance in Time

'I am constantly searching for the processes that will release good ideas from myself and the dancers. It's important that we are able to use the knowledge we have already acquired without being constrained by it. We all need to release ourselves from complacency and find motivation, and the processes that do this will sometimes relate very obviously to the theme of the piece. Other times they may not.

I like the way the human body has the ability to shift from very abstract movement to much more human expression. Human beings have a great capacity for abstract thought and expression which is, in fact, a very human characteristic.

Although the aesthetic of the finished piece is of paramount importance, I do not create work from a pictorial starting point. My first concern is always the internal workings of the movement and I find the extended possibilities this creates very exciting.' *Siobhan Davies*

By the time Siobhan Davies made *White Man Sleeps* in 1988 she had created over thirty pieces of professional choreography. In 1987 this body of work was recognised by a Fulbright Arts Fellowship, and the ensuing study visit to America provided Davies with a rare opportunity to examine her role as a choreographer. During this period she took time to think about her work and the elements that comprised it. She paid particular attention to the very essence of the movement material she created with the dancers.

▶ Choreographic Developments, pp. 13–15.

'I already understood that a dancer's training and the knowledge of the choreographer had the potential to over-influence the choreography. So I tried to look at the dancer's body as a massive resource of movement potential rather than as an exponent of a particular technique. I wanted the dancers to develop technique that was very personal to them and the full range of their movement capability, rather than a pre-defined range of movement influenced by their training. I wanted this personal technique to find the limits of the dancers and expand along with them.'

▶ Dancers, pp. 35–9.

In addition to this examination of her own ideas as a choreographer, Davies studied release technique with Nancy Topf and, perhaps more relevant to *White Man Sleeps*, she learnt about anatomy: 'While I was in New York, I went to various classes in which people discussed our anatomy and how deep within the body movement can begin. It was not only bone structure and musculature, but innards, heart, pulse and the origins of breath. It all fell into place, this extraordinary complexity of how the body is made.'

Davies was also influenced by America itself, having found a particular resonance in its relationship with those who populated it. 'Of some of the things that I learnt in America, one, which I applied more specifically to *Wyoming* [1988], was being in the middle of an American landscape, which is so much larger than anything we have in Europe, where there is human

▶ Design, p. 51.

culture everywhere. In the middle of these American landscapes, there is very little human mark. So the moment you see something human, it has a very particular heat . . . a recognition. It's a very simple idea, but it made me think very much about the body. How some simple human movement can have an extraordinary possibility and resonance to it, even simply walking.'

Upon her return from America, Davies formed Siobhan Davies Dance Company in 1988. From the outset it was important that this new company would focus on one set of work which would be developed in collaboration with the dancers. 'I wanted to ask the dancers to be decision-makers

▶ Dancers, pp. 35–9.

about how they wanted to work. It took several pieces to gain confidence in that as an idea. *White Man Sleeps* was the beginning of that process.'

The first two pieces she made with the company drew on her experiences in America in different ways. While *Wyoming* was deeply rooted in the American landscape itself, *White Man Sleeps* drew much of its inspiration from Davies's anatomical studies. 'It was the beginnings of trying to think of the body broken down and made up in far more complex forms

▶ Choreographic Developments, p. 16.

than by geometry, design, architecture or sweeping the space out.'

It is clear that by the time Davies came to make *White Man Sleeps* she had reached a crucial point in her career. Her experiences in America had impacted upon her in many different ways. She was keen to experiment with a vast number of new ideas, taken from her studies and from America itself. It was an invaluable period of self-examination.

▶ Choreographic Developments, pp. 13–15.

The reality was that *White Man Sleeps* was due to be premiered at Riverside Studios, London, in November 1988, along with *Wyoming*. With all that she had to do upon her return to Britain, Davies had only three weeks to make the new piece, and was also working with two dancers she had never worked with before (Scott Clark and Michael Fulwell). Because of this she had to translate many of her ideas into practical tasks that would enable her to start creating movement with the dancers straight away.

▶ Physical Puzzles, pp. 17–18.

'To create a starting point I devised a series of phrases which comprised movements that ran down the length of the spine. The ribcage was used as the horizontal while the hips and shoulders provided punctuation on the outside of the body.

'From this, each dancer and myself worked out a continuation which took these still very broken ideas and developed them into a liquid phrase which ended with the hands circling the head and coming together in front of the face in the form of an animal's face. Some of these ideas were borrowed from movements first explored in *Sphinx* [1977]. Into this developing choreography I began to add other ideas such as the different lengths of stride taken by the dancers which ·in some way mimicked the movement spans of different animals.

▶ Key Motifs, p. 74.

▶ Dancers, p. 37.

'Also, with Scott Clark's solo and duet with Lauren Potter, I created a movement which deliberately sought to accentuate the full length of their bodies. Particularly in the duet, Scott used the extent of his arms to measure Lauren from her heel to the top of her head. This movement was deliberately opposite in effect to the smaller movements I had been working with.

▶ Compare this with the way it was filmed. Film, p. 64.

'As far as the structure is concerned it is not over complex, and much of it takes a great deal of information from the separate movements of the music. But within that structure there are some particular placement ideas that may be worth mentioning. One of these is the way in which

▶ Music/Dance Dialogue, p. 45.

solos and duets deliberately command the space that they are in so that they not only provide a focal point, but allude to a much wider area than they occupy. The subsequent pulsing inwards deliberately defines the space that they are in.

► Film, p. 60. Introducing the Work, p. 73.

'This effect is balanced by other sections where the dancers mark the edges of the stage so that they are defining a distinct space by reaching its full extent. In the film this effect is heightened by the dancers travelling across the entire width of the screen so that there is no visible beginning and end to the movement.'

► Following the Work, pp. 91–3. Film, pp. 63–4.

As with all of Davies's work, movement was at the very heart of the development of *White Man Sleeps*. But, also in common with her other pieces, the dance was part of a larger project, incorporating music and design from the very beginning so that the finished piece was the result of a more substantial, collaborative process.

► Dialogues in Dance, pp. 33–4.

One of the first elements Davies began to work with was Kevin Volans's *White Man Sleeps*, the composition for string quartet which gave Davies's piece its own name. 'I had been listening to an enormous amount of music and in doing that I had come across a small part of Kevin's *White Man Sleeps* for string quartet. Through his agent, Chester Music, I was able to find a lot more of his work. I was able to locate him in Ireland and I called him to tell him that I was interested in using his music for my new piece. I also knew that I wanted it to be performed live, and with Kevin's music being very difficult to play it was extremely important that we found the right musicians.'

► Music, pp. 40–8.

For Davies, Volans's composition fitted in well with both her recent thoughts about her choreography and, more specifically, *White Man Sleeps* itself. 'What struck me initially about the music was that although I had heard a great deal of string quartet music before Kevin's music took the sound beyond what I was used to. It was also rhythmically engrossing and encompassed a variety of different speeds. Having recently worked with a consistent pace in the form of Steve Reich's music [for *Embarque*, 1988] this was quite a change for me and, specifically, the breaking up of the rhythms related well to my thoughts about breaking up the body into constituent parts.'

► Musical Sources, pp. 43–4.

Kevin Volans also provided one of the starting points for the design: 'Kevin showed me a book of Shoowa weavings, from Africa. What interested me about them was the way in which those patterns started with a particular intricate structure and then developed into a different pattern without any obvious logic.'

▶ Musical Sources, pp. 42–3.

The ideas that presented themselves in these Shoowa weavings formed part of the inspiration for Davies's design collaborator, David Buckland. Their most prominent influence can be seen in the painted floor for the piece, the patterns of which were greater emphasised by Peter Mumford's patchwork lighting.

▶ Designing White Man Sleeps, p. 52.

▶ Lighting, pp. 52–3.

Peter Mumford also directed the film of *White Man Sleeps*, adding another, filmic layer to the different media already present in the dance. As mentioned above, this multi-artform nature of Davies's work can be seen as one of its defining features. Davies views this collaborative process as fundamental to making the work complete for the viewer: 'The idea is to make the dancer and the dance clear for the audience to see. There need to be several layers of entry into the piece. I am constantly juggling with the paradox between creating intricate movements and the need for a big stage picture. I understand that it's quite hard to get the audience straight into a piece, and stage design can capture the audience's initial attention.

▶ Film, pp. 55–64.

▶ Interpreting the Work, pp. 105–6.

'When you take dance into the theatre, the whole experience of involving live music, performers and design allows the audience to enter into a particular world. Collaborators play a vital role in creating that place.

'I constantly make dance the chief motivator, but having chosen a collaborator the most important thing I can do is leave them alone. Because I am not a designer or a composer my ideas about these fields are naive in the same way that these artists' ideas about choreography would be. We have several conversations at the beginning of the piece in which basic needs and directions are discussed and then during the process ideas are relayed back. For all of this to work it is very important that I trust the collaborators.'

▶ Dialogues in Dance, pp. 33–4.

When discussing Davies's work as a collaborative process it is important to see that process as encompassing the dancers. Part of her motivation for creating Siobhan Davies Dance Company was the opportunity to work with experienced dancers who could play a genuine role in making the building blocks of the choreography, the movement.

Yet Davies doesn't see this method of working as resulting in roles within the piece that can only be performed by the original dancer. Rather, she wants to make sure that individual parts have been created with sufficient depth of knowledge to make them transferable, in the most part, to other dancers.

▶ Dancers, pp. 35–9.

'Initially the dancers are the lifeblood of how the piece is made. Over a period of time the dancer and I know that if a piece has been made properly then that dancer's part could be transferred to another dancer who has a different technique and experience but who will be able to embrace the geography of the movement, bringing to it their own particu-

▶ Reworkings, p. 19.

lar knowledge. Individual dancers can pick up the structure but still allow room for manoeuvre.'

Davies reworked *White Man Sleeps* in 1997. The original had been one of the first pieces made with the new ideas she had developed in America, and in the intervening nine years she developed these ideas further. Some of those developments can be understood by looking at the reworked version in comparison with the original.

'All my work goes in series where the successes and failures of a particular piece inform the one after it. To see how my work has progressed since the original *White Man Sleeps* it helps to look at the 1997 version. In this, many of the pictorial shapes were taken away in favour of a more

▶ White Man Sleeps Revisited, p. 21.

internal, visceral understanding.'

Bearing in mind that one of the *raisons d'être* of Siobhan Davies Dance Company was the continued creation of new work, it may seem strange that Davies chose to revive an earlier piece. In fact, the important point here is that the later work was not so much a revival as a reworking. Davies says that fellow choreographer Richard Alston 'has been good at getting me to re-examine work I have already made. In doing this I chose to look at *White Man Sleeps* again. All the movement was re-examined. The scoring for string quartet that was used was changed in favour of Kevin's

▶ White Man Sleeps Revisited, pp. 47–8.

earlier arrangement for prepared harpsichords, viola da gamba and percussion. This particular arrangement was more raw and I felt that it would cause both myself and the audience to re-examine the piece.'

The reworked version of *White Man Sleeps* toured throughout 1997. The differences between this version and the original genuinely highlight the development in Davies's choreography in the intervening years, and anticipate her continuing growth as a choreographer.

Part 2
Contexts

Sarah Whatley

The place of White Man Sleeps in Davies's career, and in the context of contemporary dance in Britain

Michael Fulwell, Lauren Potter.
(Part 1, Section A.)
Photo: David Buckland.

Choreographic Developments

Well before *White Man Sleeps*, Davies had already established a critical reputation as a prolific choreographer, and many writers have documented her progress to that point, identifying different phases of development in her choreographic career. The year before *White Man Sleeps*, 1987, turned out to be a significant one for Davies: she took a year out from work, travelling to the US with her family, funded by the first Fulbright Arts Fellowship in Choreography. She describes this as a period of reassessment, rediscovery, and a chance to feed, stimulate and extend her imagination. On her return, she choreographed several works for Rambert Dance Company, formed Siobhan Davies Dance Company, and began what can be described as another phase in her choreographic career.

→ See, for example, Clarke and Crisp, *London Contemporary Dance Theatre*; Jordan, *Striding Out*, Ch. 6; Kane, 'Siobhan Davies: Family Connections'; Mackrell, 'Siobhan Davies'; Sanders, *Siobhan Davies: The Development of a Choreographic Style*.

It is possible to trace many reasons for this new phase in Davies's work, and undoubtedly her experiences in the US, combined with her own growth as an artist, are significant factors. However, by examining the general context in which this work was first seen, we are better able to understand the development evident in her work, and the reaction and response it received from audiences and critics in Britain at this time.

Prior to 1987

By the mid-1980s, there was already something of a tension in Davies's work. A brief survey of her choreographic output at this time suggests she was searching for change and a more appropriate context and environment in which to develop her work. Davies was combining her work as Resident Choreographer with London Contemporary Dance Theatre (LCDT) with making work on a smaller scale with Second Stride, which gave her the opportunity to choreograph more work, experiment creatively

→ Jordan, *Striding Out*, pp. 132–3.

and take more choreographic risks. Also at this time she stopped performing herself and needed a new direction for her energies and creativity. This shift brought about a period of reflection. Her choreography for LCDT was showing signs of becoming creatively tired, and perhaps more clearly than before, Davies began to exhibit a desire to work again on a more intimate scale, in a more collaborative way with the dancers, drawing more from their own creativity and movement ideas to realise her own vision.

Davies's interest in working in partnership with dancers, as interpreters of her ideas, can be traced back to her experience of working with Namron on *Sphinx* (1977), with LCDT. But by the mid-1980s, as a large repertory company, LCDT demanded that the dancers were able to work with a plurality of dance styles, and rehearsal periods frequently required dancers to work on more than one piece at a time, thus limiting the dancers' own contribution to the working process of any one choreographic approach, and giving Davies the chance to make only one work each year. Both *Silent Partners*, choreographed by Davies for Second Stride in 1984, and *Bridge the Distance*, choreographed for LCDT in 1985, can be seen as poignant, reflective, deeply personal statements and as precursors for change. While these works have a narrative basis, Davies was already exploring more closely the essence of her movement vocabulary and considering ways in which the human condition could be best communicated in dance.

The works Davies choreographed for LCDT just prior to her departure from the company in 1987 – *The Run to Earth, and do they do* (both 1986), and *Red Steps* (1987) – demonstrate how Davies was already asking for more from dancers she was working with. Set to Michael Nyman's minimalist score, *and do they do* required a fleet-footedness and a fluency of weight which the company, unaccustomed to such demands, had problems with; and both *The Run to Earth* and *and do they do* contain clues to what would be revealed more vividly in later work – 'an unusual consideration for the territories and spatial implications of the stage, and for links between her contribution and the design and lighting introduced by her regular collaborators David Buckland and Peter Mumford'. *Red Steps*, her second work to a score by minimalist composer John Adams (the first

▶ Dancers, pp. 37–8.

→ See also Preston, 'Beyond Words'.

→ Jordan, 'Siobhan Davies: Two for LCDT', p. 14

→ Jordan, 'Siobhan Davies: Two for LCDT', p. 12

was *New Galileo*, 1984), is another study of pure dance, yet shows a heightened consideration for phrasing and pace with a spatial juxtaposition of stillness with hectic activity. It seemed Davies was leaving LCDT just when the company was most in need of her choreographic talent.

Davies's preference for working with mature and experienced dancers at this time – seen in Patrick Harding-Irmer's extended solo in *Bridge the Distance*, and the duet for Lauren Potter and Darshan Singh Bhuller in *The Run to Earth* – was significant in the selection of dancers for her own company in 1988 and the subsequent development of a movement technique which would serve as a method to develop and challenge trained dancers, rather than as a way of training younger, less experienced dancers. Davies's departure from Britain in 1987 was at a critical time, both in terms of her own future development as a choreographer and the future of mainstream British contemporary dance as a whole.

● Task 1, p. 29.

▶ Dialogues in Dance, pp. 34–5.

An American Sabbatical

Davies's trip to America in 1987 enabled her to spend a significant period of time reflecting on her own work, reading work by American writers, and absorbing from the American environment and landscape. She has spoken about this visit at length, about the people, the time with her family, the sense of freedom, and the three-dimensionality of the American landscape.

→ Ensor, 'A Novel Approach to Dance'.

Davies was also able to reassess her own working practices and the technical basis for her work by taking classes with a range of dancers and teachers. The focus of her training was release techniques, Alexander technique, and other movement classes. Alexander technique teaches students to become aware of their own habitual movement patterns: to unlearn, not do, or inhibit those patterns and substitute new ones. Teachers are trained how to communicate kinaesthetic information through touch. Davies has spoken of the way she 'learnt to think of the body in much smaller units – in terms of tiny joints; in terms of subtle placing of the weight, in terms of what the focus of the eye could do to the face'.

→ For an introductory explanation of 'release' see the glossary in Mackrell, *Out of Line*.

→ On Alexander Technique, see Alexander, *The Use of the Self*. On Karczag, see Jordan, *Striding Out*, and Karczag, *The Constructive Rest Position*.

→ Mackrell, 'Stories in Dance'.

Return to Britain

When Davies returned in 1988 she was able to combine working with her own small company of dancers with working on a larger scale, choreographing for Rambert Dance Company (she was appointed Associate Choreographer for the company in 1989). The four works she created for Rambert – *Embarque* (1988), *Sounding* (1989), *Signature* (1990) and *Winnsboro Cotton Mill Blues* (1992) – all contain clear influences from her experiences in America. The Rambert dancers were invited to contribute their own movement material, and make personal statements, a way of working that was unfamiliar to this company at the time. *Embarque*, to music by American composer Steve Reich, has a sense of place and travel, an exhilarating energy and, as suggested by the title, an idea of setting out on a new venture. *Sounding* has a primordial quality, exploring gravity and giving in to weight. In *Winnsboro Cotton Mill Blues*, Davies used music of the same name as a starting point (the fourth and last of the *North American Ballads* for solo piano by American composer Frederic Rzewski). Industrialisation and its effects on people provide the theme for this piece. By contrast, the more abstract *Signature* is developed from the dancers' own personal movement 'signatures', suggesting a community ritual.

In a similar way, each work she made for her own company during this time – in particular *Wyoming, White Man Sleeps* (both 1988), *Cover Him with Grass, Drawn Breath* (both 1989) and *Different Trains* (1990) – makes some reference, in music, movement or subject matter, to another culture. Although showing a sense of freedom, with bold and generous use of space, the movement material in these works is predominantly soft, fluid and liquid, exploring subtle articulations in the body, with a quiet intimacy and unprojected outward focus. Initially, Davies worked with writing by American author Gretel Ehrlich for *Wyoming*, also commissioning text from her for *Arctic Heart* (1991); but perhaps in a more subtle way her movement vocabulary at this time evolved predominantly through the use of imagery to generate material, and a technical basis which drew on principles of release techniques, contact improvisation and other American-grown approaches to dance development.

▶ A Dance in Time, p. 4.

→ Ehrlich, *The Solace of Open Spaces*.

Physical Puzzles

By 1992, Davies's energies seemed clearly directed towards her own company and making work on a more intimate scale. Davies had moved further away from narratives and dramatic ideas in her dances, favouring her interest in solving, or setting for her dancers to solve, a physical or spatial challenge, riddle or puzzle as a way of 'unlocking' new material, thereby enriching her movement vocabulary with each new work. Such a concern is seen in *Make Make* (1992), where the dancers were set the task of finding out how a phrase performed in the upper body could be performed with a phrase made for the lower body, thus finding themselves in less usual places, performing less simply co-ordinated material.

● Task 2, p. 29.

Wild Translations (1995) explored movement which was deliberately contradictory to the natural or easy inclination (for example, moving the

Rehearsal photograph showing a movement canon in the opening part of the work.
Left to right: Scott Clark, Lauren Potter, Paul Douglas, Michael Fulwell, Catherine Quinn.
(Part 1, Section C.)
Photo: David Buckland

top of the head and tailbone in opposition). *The Art of Touch* (1995), the companion piece in that programme, is another study in contrasts and opposites, but also marks another subtle shift in her work. There is more speed than in Davies's previous works, more outward focus, a more extravagant, overt sense of theatricality, which draws attention to the dancers' technical skills. The dancers respond to the sound and complexity of the music, focusing in particular on the rhythmic structures produced by the feet and legs to make flamboyant, dextrous movement.

▶ White Man Sleeps
Revisited, p. 47.

More recently, in making *Eighty Eight* (1998), Davies presented a series of tasks or events to the dancers by numbering body parts and making conversations between two or more of them, while also reflecting the rhythms and physicality of the music. Only two works have dealt more directly with issues or stories: *Different Trains*, dressed in everyday clothes, responded to the text in Steve Reich's music, and *Wanting To Tell Stories* (1993) developed out of the expressive and narrative potential of gesture. Both these pieces are suggestive and reminiscent of people in relationships, rather than explicitly about particular events or experiences.

Spatial Territories and New Music

Other starting points Davies has used include a range of different music and design. On many occasions she has collaborated with designers David Buckland (who travelled through America with Davies) and Peter Mumford to enhance meaning by creating spatial pathways and a more sharply focused sense of territory on stage. In *Wanting to Tell Stories*, two enormous screens hang, rotate and slide to divide and close off areas of the stage, providing intimate and open spaces, corridors, private and public rooms.

▶ Designing for Dance,
p. 49.

In *Trespass* (1996) design had a more significant role by literally trespassing into the dancers' space. Davies began the piece by inviting Buckland to design constructions as extensions to the dancers' bodies, and structures or props which the dancers would need to negotiate and manipulate within the piece.

Much of Davies's work over the last decade demonstrates her continued interest in collaborations with composers. She has used a wide range of music, including harpsichord sonatas by Scarlatti juxtaposed with Matteo Fargion's *Sette Canzoni* for *The Art of Touch*, as well as scores by minimalist composers; but has worked in collaboration most often with Kevin Volans, creating six pieces to his music. These eclectic musical choices have challenged her own creativity and response to sound and texture. She encourages her dancers to really know the music, often allowing them to find their own phrasing and points of contact with the music. In this way the dance can develop its own shape and rhythm while avoiding competing with the music.

▶ Dancers, p. 37. Music/Dance Dialogue, p. 46.

● Task 3, p. 29.

Reworkings

By 1995, although still comparatively small, Davies's company had grown in number from five to seven dancers; but from the original members only Gill Clarke had remained throughout. Davies had already developed a new choreographic style which was becoming possible to identify, and a working method which grew out of a shared company 'language', a way of generating, shaping and discussing movement material. At this time, Davies began to revisit earlier works. Her intention has never been to reconstruct the original work faithfully, step by step, but rather to recreate the work to explore how her own ideas have grown and changed over time, and how those who she is working with can make the dance 'their own'.

▶ A Dance in Time, p. 8.

She began in 1995 by looking again at *Sphinx*, originally choreographed for London Contemporary Dance Theatre in 1977, this time setting it on 4D, the graduate company of London Contemporary Dance School. Although the work is recognisably 'the same', the choreography has many changes, reflecting the changes to the dancers' training and Davies's own experience of contact improvisation and release methods. Reconstructing the piece from video and memory meant that some sections were lost. Davies choreographed new material, which explored soft partnering material and movement which flows seamlessly and fluidly, with less emphasis on end positions and body design.

Gill Clarke in the 1997
version of White Man Sleeps.
Photo: Sean Hudson

Linked Programmes

Another important choreographic statement came the following year, in 1996, when Davies rehearsed and toured two works in tandem: *Trespass* and *Affections*. Ideas in *Trespass*, the earlier work, are revisited, repeated and sometimes changed in *Affections*. *Trespass* has all the distinctive features of a Davies work: highly charged dance which luxuriates in its physical substance and presence. Loose-limbed, generous, full-bodied, yet quirky, *Trespass* is a series of short episodes in which the dancers collide and disperse, and shows another fruitful companionship between music and movement. Davies's dance does not simply illustrate Gerald Barry's music; and the music does not so much trespass on the dancers' world as steer, direct and impel the dancers on. The height and scale of *Trespass* is echoed in *Affections*, but whereas in *Trespass* ideas splintered, came to an abrupt end and were raced through, *Affections* takes more time, expanding earlier ideas into more personal statements. So 'sentences', often incomplete in the earlier work, became 'chapters'. *Affections* is in complete contrast to *Trespass*, yet while there are clear differences in mood and atmosphere, in both works the movement does not so much represent ideas or emotions but suggests and evokes qualities and images.

White Man Sleeps Revisited

In 1997, nearly ten years after the original choreography, Davies revisited *White Man Sleeps*. She reworked some of the original choreography, and this time set the work to Volans's earlier instrumentation of *White Man Sleeps* (1982), for harpsichords, viola da gamba and percussion. In this way, Davies's reinvention of the work can be seen to reflect a similar process to that of the composer, although Davies chose to work with the later arrangement of the music first. This version of *White Man Sleeps* became less about the imagery which inspired Davies initially, and more about the relationship between the dance and music, and the weight and physicality of the movement itself.

▶ A Dance in Time, p. 8.

Performed by a largely new cast (Gill Clarke and Catherine Quinn were the only surviving members of the original company ensemble), the movement reflects the harder edged texture of the music. The fluidity, complexity and spatial patterning is still present but the phrasing is different, and the movement seems bigger, more shaped, more percussive. There is some new material, including a new section, and Scott Clark's role, as a more distinct individual within the piece, disappears. Even though much of the choreography is similar, if not the same, the overall effect is that the work looks and feels different, less settled and at ease.

▶ White Man Sleeps Revisited, pp. 47–8.

● Task 4, p. 29.

Accompanying *White Man Sleeps* at this time was *Bank*, another collaboration between Davies, Buckland and Fargion, who provided a dense and highly rhythmic, percussive score. This time the spatial complexity is created by the dancers colliding, interlocking then separating. There is a feeling of unrest, of fragmentation, as dancers are at times isolated then driven back into the group by forces beyond their control. Davies's return to America later in the year with her company, to perform *Bank* alongside *The Art of Touch*, ten years after the visit which propelled Davies into such a prolific period of work, marked another 'coming of age' and met with enthusiastic response from the New York critics.

Looking Forward

● Task 5, p. 29.

▶ On Volans, see Music, pp. 40–2.

In 1998, to celebrate ten years of her own company, Davies expanded the company to ten dancers and reworked *Winnsboro Cotton Mill Blues*, originally made for Rambert Dance Company, to tour alongside a new work, *Eighty Eight*. As in the previous year, Davies worked on developing a programme of companion pieces by having clear links in either mood or thematic content. But here, in *Eighty Eight*, Davies set herself a new challenge. Set to a sequence of studies for pianola by Conlon Nancarrow, the complexity and invention of the dancers' movement seems almost as impossible for the human body as the music is for human hands to play. The breathtaking energy of this piece is set within an urban, industrial environment of steaming metallic pipes and moving lights. *Winnsboro*

Cotton Mill Blues continues the theme of hard, strenuous work as the dancers dive through space to Rzewski's piano music, then line up for busy, rhythmic, work-like actions, reflecting the mechanistic and repetitive qualities of industrial looms.

In 1999, now with a company of eight dancers, the aptly titled *Wild Air* marked Davies's first full-evening work. In some ways it is a return to the quieter, more contemplative work from ten years previously; and yet there is an extraordinary sense of lightness and of flight in the dancing. This time there are subtle references to Japanese art in the set design and the crisp white costumes. With music by her frequent collaborator, Kevin Volans, the work has moments of surprising quietness and long held stillness. Enigmatic in parts, yet without ever becoming obscure, this is silky, vibrant dancing, with Davies's familiar attention to the smallest detail.

In July 1999, Davies was commissioned by Artangel to direct *13 Different Keys*, a site-specific, promenade performance at the Atlantis Gallery in Brick Lane, London. Working in collaboration with regular lighting designer Peter Mumford, Deborah Bull, principal artist at the Royal Ballet, Gill Clarke and three other dancers, Davies brought classical ballet and contemporary dance together to explore the unique architectural qualities of the top floor of the building. Her next commission, a new work for the Royal Ballet in December 1999, at the refurbished Royal Opera House, promises to be another new adventure, although working with unknown dancers, over a short period of time, means Davies will have little time for 'process', for her usual playful exploration of movement material.

Summary

■ Since 1988, Davies has worked on a project basis, bringing her small ensemble of dancers together for two rehearsal and touring periods each year. Although the company line-up has changed over time, many dancers have stayed with the company for a number of years.

▶ Dialogues in Dance, pp. 33–4.

■ Fundamental to the success of her work is her commitment to working collaboratively and democratically with her dancers, and also with composers and designers.

■ As a result, much of the movement material is highly individual, developed by the dancers themselves, and the company style is developed collectively with her dancers, past and present.

■ In the continuing evolution of her choreographic style, Davies believes in a rigorous exploration and investigation of movement, and its power to say more about being human.

Contemporary Dance in Britain

A number of British dancers and choreographers have visited America for creative stimulation, which has often brought about changes in British dance as a whole. By looking at the different phases of Davies's choreographic development, it is possible to see that each visit she made to America has been an important catalyst for change. In 1976, Davies visited to study primarily Cunningham technique at the Cunningham Studio, and classical ballet. This resulted in work which explored alternative ways of moving to the Graham-based style of her early training and led to her working more collaboratively with her dancers, seen first most clearly in *Step at a Time* (1976). *Sphinx* (1977) marked the first clear turning point in her movement vocabulary, away from body design towards motion as the driving force for her movement invention. Davies's extended visit to America during 1987 brought about the most significant and distinct changes in her work. In some ways, the work Davies made on her return showed a clarity and purpose that had certainly been suggested or hinted at in her earlier choreography, but had never before been so clear. In other ways, it brought to 'mainstream' contemporary dance a movement philosophy and approach to generating and performing dance material which had previously been aligned to the working methods of the New Dance movement in British dance, which had quite a different path of development to that of mainstream contemporary dance.

→ For an introductory explanation to Cunningham and Graham techniques, see the glossary in Mackrell, *Out of Line*.

▶ Dancers, p. 35.

● Task 6, p. 29.

● Task 7, p. 29.

By the end of the 1980s, the New Dance movement in Britain had itself come of age. The work of the X6 Collective, who initiated the publication of *New Dance* magazine, can in some ways be seen to have direct parallels with the Judson Dance Theater movement in the US in the 1960s, in terms of bringing together dancers and other artists who were looking to alternative ways of training, presenting and performing dance which encouraged exploration and alternatives to hierarchical methods and structures. In

→ See Banes, *Terpsichore in Sneakers*; Novack, *Sharing the Dance*.

other ways, the work of the X6 Collective established for the first time a clear British movement in dance and set the agenda for future developments and support structures for dancers by giving them a collective 'voice'. The ten years of the New Dance movement was a rich period for establishing awareness, support and respect for independent dance activity in Britain; but by the end of the 1980s, landmark events effectively drew a close to this important phase.

→ On New Dance, see Jordan, *Striding Out*; Mackrell, *Out of Line*.

● Task 8, p. 29.

Mainstream Contemporary Dance

By the mid-1980s, large-scale 'mainstream' British contemporary dance was reaching something of a crisis point. Rapidly changing patterns in both participation in dance and attendance at dance performances during the 1970s and early 1980s had led to concerns to devise a strategy to ensure the future of professional dance in Britain. At the end of 1988 Graham Devlin was commissioned by the Arts Council's Dance Department to undertake research into the future of dance in Britain, resulting in the *Stepping Forward* report. Devlin found that audiences for the major contemporary dance companies, LCDT and Rambert Dance Company, had declined by a third during the early eighties, and 1985/86 saw a further alarming decrease. Furthermore, the dance works were generally regarded as elitist, inaccessible, cool and passionless. The report called for a radical reassessment and suggested there was a void in the dance spectrum, with a gap in 'middle-scale' companies offering acknowledged quality and a distinctive identity. This unsettling context for the leading contemporary dance companies can be seen to have provided an opportunity for Davies and her new company, in 1988, to offer something of a solution to the problem, by injecting a new vitality and a new focus within middle-scale dance.

→ Devlin, *Stepping Forward*, pp. 66–8.

Other, unrelated events also played a significant role in the formation of Davies's new company. Janet Smith and Dancers had disbanded due to financial difficulties, which enabled company member Gill Clarke to perform in the opening programme of Davies's new company, standing in for Lizie Saunderson who had sustained an injury in the days leading up to the premiere. Gill Clarke became an important, long-standing member of the company, maintaining an unbroken relationship with the company until 1998.

New Dance Influences

Davies's new work for her own company in 1988 came at a time when dancers, audiences and critics were poised for something new. Davies was already well established and respected within the culture of major, mainstream contemporary dance; but now, through her use of choreographic methods which grew out of anatomically sound movement principles, safe and efficient body use, and greater respect for the individual's contribution to the working process, her work appeared to embody principles which had previously been more obviously associated with dance practitioners from within the New Dance movement. Richard Alston, a close colleague, also believed that when Davies stopped performing, the passion she displayed as a performer was released into her choreography. Critics who had struggled with the restraint of her earlier work, in particular her more 'narrative' works, responded well to the physicality and sensuality in the new work.

→ Jordan, *Striding Out*, p. 140.

The early stages of her own company, and the dancers she selected to form that company, secured a clear movement philosophy and a firm foundation upon which the future direction of her work was based. At this point, Davies initiated the physical exploration of her new movement vocabulary, supported and to some extent guided by her dancers, in particular the American dancer and Feldenkrais practitioner Scott Clark, who led many company classes and introduced image-based movement explorations to the company's working methods. Davies had by this time established a mutually respectful relationship between herself and her dancers. In this way she was able to create a 'community' of dancers, a 'family unit' which offered source material for her choreography as well as serving as a support structure for herself, her work and the company of dancers themselves.

▶ Dancers, p. 38.

→ Feldenkrais technique introduces a series of movements which work to affect a particular muscle group by working with its antagonists rather than with agonists. For further reading see Feldenkrais, *Awareness Through Movement*.

Summary

In identifying trends, patterns and key people that may have been signifi-cant in influencing Davies's new choreographic phase since 1988, the following points can be considered:

■ Dance in Britain in the late 1980s was in a transitional stage. Funding for dance companies was under threat and it was clear that the scale and nature of work could not be sustained without substantial increases in funding. The major contemporary dance companies were particularly vul-nerable. It was thought that there was little quality work in the middle scale, and dance needed an injection of fresh energy, combined with a renewed accessibility to recover audiences.

■ Davies's period of study in America can therefore be seen as timely, both for her own invigoration as a choreographer and for British dance as a whole. Once more, her American experiences brought about another cycle in her choreography which both responded to and helped to create a new phase in British dance.

■ The clarity and integrity in Davies's richly complex yet refined move-ment vocabulary called for a new way of looking at dance and writing about dance, which demanded greater attention to the movement itself.

■ The dancers, some of whom were known or became known as in-dependent dancers in their own right, undoubtedly played a significant role in establishing the quality and success of Davies's work.

■ The company's work filled a gap in the middle scale, with a repertoire choreographed by Davies alone, which ensured a clear stylistic voice and identity.

● Task 9, p. 29.
Task 10, p. 29.

Tasks

1. With reference to your own experience of choreographing and watching dances, describe the many different ways that a choreographer can involve the dancers in the creative process.

2. Devise a movement phrase which explores ways of moving the arms and upper body. Devise another for the legs and lower body. Co-ordinate the two phrases (a) in a harmonious way, and (b) in a disjointed way. What rhythmical patterns emerge? What are the connotations given by the movements?

3. Collaboration can take many forms. How can all members of a creative team be equal collaborators? Explore the ways in which different artists can work together on a project to make a dance work.

4. What are the different purposes of reviving a dance? Would they lead to a reconstruction, or a recreation? Discuss the possible approaches you could take to reviving *White Man Sleeps*, depending on the motives for the revival. Which aspects of the piece would you keep the same, and which would you change? Are the changes by choice or necessity?

5. Consider the reconstruction of dance works. Argue the case for choreographers either faithfully reconstructing their own work as closely as possible to the original, or remaking the work with changes as they wish.

6. Describe the key principles which underpin Martha Graham's technique and Merce Cunningham's technique. Identify moments in *White Man Sleeps* which either clearly relate to, or are in direct contrast to these principles.

7. Contemporary dance in Britain owes much to America. Discuss.

8. What was X6? Which artists were associated with X6? What evidence can you find to support the notion that the legacy of X6 is highly visible in British dance today?

9. Davies is undoubtedly one of Britain's most respected choreographers. How does her work compare with other women choreographers working in British dance today? What conclusions can you draw?

10. It could be said that dance in Britain is dominated by male choreographers. Do you agree or disagree? Argue the case for your point of view.

Part 3
Collaborations

Sanjoy Roy

Paul Douglas

The different media of the dance,
and the contributions of the dancers,
composer, designers and film director

Dialogues in Dance

The process by which a dance is made is integral to the final outcome, affecting not only how it is created, but also what is created and how it is performed. Davies's preferred working process can be described as one of *collaboration* and *dialogue*, and its effects can be seen in the finished dance itself.

At the beginning of the rehearsal process, Davies rarely has any fixed ideas about the outcome. Rather, she begins with *points of departure* (general images, starting points, outlines, physical puzzles) and works through these in dialogue with her collaborators: the dancers perhaps most importantly, the composer (if the music is commissioned) and the set, costume and lighting designers. The collaborators thus contribute to the final piece both separately and together, and often Davies is more interested in the richness of the effects that emerge from this dialogue than in the expression of a single intention.

▶ Physical Puzzles, pp. 17–18.

▶ A Dance in Time, p. 7.

As Davies says, this method of working allows her ideas 'to accumulate into something better than the original idea'. It also means that the final piece becomes a web of different interplays between dancers, music and design which are not necessarily organised to express a single idea: sometimes they work separately, sometimes in congruence or in counterpoint, and the focus will shift between them during the performance.

▶ Elements of the Work, pp. 69–71.

→ Volans, 'A Dialogue Between Collaborators'.

● Task 1. p. 65.

In a sense, too, the viewers become the final collaborators in making the dance meaningful: instead of being asked to 'decipher' the work to arrive at a 'correct' interpretation, they are invited into a dialogue with the piece, to register the dance's fluctuating effects and to contribute their own personal responses.

▶ Interpreting the Work, pp. 105–6.

● Task 2, p. 65.

Because the collaborators contribute to the work both separately and together, Davies often prefers to work with experienced artists, who have their own ideas and areas of interest to contribute. Similarly, she often

▶ Choreographic Developments, p. 15.

works with regular collaborators because they already have a common ground, a shared history of exploration and creation which allows them quickly to reach a point of communicative dialogue together.

Perhaps the most important collaborators are the dancers themselves. Below (pp. 35–9), dancer Paul Douglas gives his own account of working on *White Man Sleeps*. Following this are sections on the music (pp. 40–8), the set, costume and lighting design (pp. 49–54), and finally a section on filming the piece (pp. 55–64).

Dancers

Paul Douglas was one of the founder members of Siobhan Davies Dance Company in 1988, and created one of the roles in *White Man Sleeps*. He had previously danced with London Contemporary Dance Theatre, and had worked with Davies there on *Bridge the Distance*. Here, he give his own account of working with Davies on *White Man Sleeps*.

'It was very exciting being asked to be a founder member of the new company. I felt like a pioneer setting out for new territory, and it could not have come at a more fortuitous moment. Coincidentally, both Sue [Siobhan Davies] and I had not long returned from sabbaticals abroad. Sue had been to the States on a Fulbright Fellowship, and I had been to Japan with support from the Dancer's Resettlement Fund. We were both looking for a fresh start and a change of direction.

While in Japan studying Aikido with the late Seigo Yamaguchi, I had experienced a change in perception of myself and my understanding of movement. So I was pleased when we had a letter from Sue asking us *not* to take dance classes prior to starting with her. She wanted to begin with a clear palette, and that felt completely right to me.

Sue taught classes which consisted of very simple rolling exercises on the floor, and some simple shifts of weight standing up. She wanted us to really relax, to soften and open the body, and to build sensory awareness, acknowledging even the smallest fluctuations in weight and energy. This was very different from my previous dance training in the Graham and Cunningham techniques, which are rather tensile and more concerned with the arrangement of external form. It was, however, very similar to the physical orientation with which master Yamaguchi imbued his Aikido.

Sue wanted us to keep the body in an open state when researching material for the choreography. She set choreographic tasks and encour-

▶ Contemporary Dance in Britain, p. 25.

Paul Douglas and Catherine Quinn in rehearsal.
(Part 2, Section B).
Photo: David Buckland

aged us to explore them in a very personal way. We were asked to experiment with animal imagery, to imagine having a hoof instead of a foot, or a wing instead of an arm, and to mix several animals in one body. The idea was not so much to imitate these animals as to allow these images to stimulate different qualities of movement and different rhythms. I felt able to be quite instinctive, allowing whatever occurred to me to come out. We were given time to edit and arrange the material into concise phrases. We also learned each other's phrases, and were allowed some flexibility in interpretation. There were no overt rules set by Sue, but there was an expectation for us to be inventive. We deliberately avoided any known movement. There were, for instance, no arrangements of the arms originating from any formal technique. I began to experiment with movement influenced by my Aikido training, which Sue encouraged. We were discovering a new vocabulary, one specific to the intentions of this work.

● Task 3, p. 65.

▶ A Dance in Time, p. 5.

▶ Movement, p. 72.

In creating the movement, the music was, of course, a source of great inspiration. The first time I heard the score was on the stereo in Lauren Potter's car. The rhythms in the opening section reminded me of Irish jigs and reels: they had a similar vigour. The warmth and vibrancy of the music evoked an immediate physical response from me. I had to dance to it. During rehearsals we would listen to a passage of the score and then improvise with the feelings and rhythms still resonating within us. We were attempting to find ways of expressing the spirit of the music while discovering movement that was absorbing in itself. Sue always aimed for a dialogue with the score, something much more than being simply illustrative. Later, the movement would be adjusted and set more clearly to the musical framework. Sue was always clear about the juxtapositioning of movement against music, without being pedantic or rigid. The dancers would also frequently make suggestions as to how a phrase of the dance could be reinterpreted to achieve a confluence with the music. There would even be the occasional debate about how a passage of the music should be interpreted, all with the aim of finding the most satisfying resolution.

▶ Music/Dance Dialogue, pp. 44–7.

▶ Spatial Territories and New Music, p. 19. Music/Dance Dialogue, p. 46.

All of the choreographers I had worked with in London Contemporary Dance Theatre had invented movement and wanted input from the dancers, but the pressure of the working schedule (often we would work on three dances by different choreographers in the same day) meant that time for in-depth exploration was limited, and it was difficult to switch style and approach several times a day and still remain empathetic with each choreographer's needs. Also, in a large company such as LCDT (with 22 dancers) it was not easy to feel that one's personal input during the creative process had much impact on the company's development.

▶ Choreographic Developments, p. 14.

When we began with Sue in 1988, we were five dancers. That every one contributed to the development of the choreography was a vital and integral part of the process. I felt Sue trusted and respected her dancers and that she was genuinely intrigued by what we came up with. At the same time I felt highly motivated by her ideas and admired the intelligence and imagination she employed in shaping and directing the work. It felt quite luxurious to have the time and space to immerse oneself in such an intense creative process with a single choreographer, and to be able to follow it through to its fruition.

It was a wonderful group of dancers, and I took inspiration from watching the others during the creative process and in performance. Lizie Saunderson and Lauren Potter I knew from LCDT; Lauren and I had also been partners in Sue's *Bridge the Distance* for the company. Michael Fulwell was the unassuming bright new star from London Contemporary Dance

▶ The Dancers, p. 70.

School's performance group. Scott Clark was the odd one out, having no connection with our otherwise shared background.

Yet Scott was a great liberating influence on the company. He did not have the same drilling in formal techniques as the rest of us. He introduced ideas from the Feldenkrais method, a movement system which

▶ New Dance Influences, p. 27.

promotes greater awareness of bodily articulation and builds co-ordination through fascinating physical conundrums. He had also been influenced by a teacher of the Laban technique who had adapted her method for the benefit of people with disabilities. He had built into his body quite a unique network of connections. More than this, he did not have the same aesthetic parameters, and he certainly provoked me into reconsidering what I had accepted as the boundaries of dance.

The work that we produced was more fluid and idiosyncratic than anything else I had been involved in. It was grounded and sensual. It was replete with animal imagery while remaining essentially human. The dance lived and breathed with the music. There was nothing mechanical about it.

▶ Music, pp. 40, 41. Designing White Man Sleeps, p. 52.

One week prior to the premiere, disaster struck – just like in the old musical movies. Lizie and I were rehearsing a duet from *Wyoming*, the companion work to *White Man Sleeps*, and we mistimed a rather spectacular lift. Lizie hit her foot on the ground and it broke in several places. We were devastated. With one week to go and *White Man Sleeps* still to complete, Gill Clarke and Cathy Quinn stepped in to save the day. They were both incredibly quick in acquiring the movement, and were sensitive to the atmosphere of the work. I think by this point in the creative process we had established a distinctive focus to the dance that was infectious. Sue kept her calm throughout, and continued to be uncompromisingly rigorous in her decision-making.

▶ The Dancers, pp. 69–70.

When it came to performing, each of us had a considerable share of the responsibility for conveying the meanings and feelings of the work. The expectations on us were high, both from Sue and from audiences; at the same time the dance was extremely engaging and enjoyable to do. *White Man Sleeps* received an overwhelmingly enthusiastic response, which was very moving, and gave us all a tremendous sense of achievement.'

→ For more on dancers' input, see Roy, 'Making a Dance'.

Music

White Man Sleeps is named after its music, a composition by Kevin Volans made in 1982. Volans, who now lives in Ireland, was born and grew up in South Africa (where he returned from 1982 to 1984), and spent several years in Germany (1973–81), where he studied with and later became a teaching assistant to the influential avant-garde composer Karlheinz Stockhausen. Stockhausen is perhaps the best known of a generation of post-war composers who were experimenting with serialism (a compositional method based on systems, rules and formal transformations), and exploring technologies for producing electronic, synthesised and recorded sounds.

During the late 1970s, Volans made a field trip to Africa, researching and recording its sounds and music. Returning to Germany, he began to turn away from the methods of his training by incorporating some of the ideas of composition, tuning, rhythm and instrumentation he had re-encountered in Africa.

In fact, one important African influence was not music, but textiles, particularly the Shoowa designs (from Zaire). These textiles are based on repeated geometric patterns, but include an idea of spontaneity, change and even capriciousness: a pattern may be repeated at much larger size, or broken down, altered or added to as the weaver progresses. For Volans, these represented a way of composing that was both patterned and free, an order that also encompassed chaos, and which bore the physical traces of its human origin and the vagaries of the creator's imagination. So while there is a sense of unifying design, it is not a closed one: it also affords a freedom and unpredictability – 'the exact opposite of machine-made car-

▶ Designing White Man
Sleeps, p. 52.

pets,' as Volans says. It is, too, the opposite of the systematic, conceptualist techniques that he had studied in Germany.

White Man Sleeps was composed in 1982, following two earlier African-influenced pieces, *Mbira* and *Matepe*. Volans chose the title from 'a moment in *nyanga* panpipe music where the performers leave off playing their loud pipes for a few cycles and dance only to the sound of their ankle rattles, to let the white landowner sleep – for a minute or two.'

→ CD sleeve note.
▶ Music, p. 70.
● Task 4, p. 65.

A suite of five movements, it was scored for two harpsichords, viola da gamba and percussion – the harpsichords and viola da gamba being chosen partly because they could easily be retuned to an African system. Later, David Harrington, leader of the Kronos Quartet, asked Volans to rescore *White Man Sleeps* for string quartet (two violins, viola and cello). Initially reluctant to substitute the African tuning with the Western system (equal temperament), he decided that it would nevertheless be an interesting project – at least partly because he enjoyed the idea of the string quartet, a classical Western sound *par excellence*, being 'invaded' by African ideas.

Catherine Quinn, in Part 2.
Photo: David Buckland

(Volans was not trying to evoke the sounds and sights of Africa – which he would consider as 'airport art' – but to incorporate their influence into his own compositions.) For the string quartet version, he also changed the order of the movements, and replaced one of the original sections with a completely new one.

The string quartet version of *White Man Sleeps* was made in 1986, and it was this version that Davies originally heard, shortly after her return from America in 1987. For the stage performances, the score was performed live on stage by the Degas Quartet (later renamed the Smith Quartet). *White Man Sleeps* was the first time Davies used Volans's music, but she has since worked with his music for *Cover Him With Grass* (1989) and *Wild Translations* (1995), and has also commissioned scores from him for *Signature* (1990), *Wanting to Tell Stories* (1993) and *Wild Air* (1999). She also reworked *White Man Sleeps* in 1997 to the original scoring for harpsichords, viola da gamba and percussion.

For Volans, *White Man Sleeps* was the first of his scores used for dance, but his music has since been used by many choreographers internationally, although his closest collaborations to date have been with Davies, Jonathan Burrows, and Shobana Jeyasingh.

Musical Sources

For *White Man Sleeps*, Davies was using an existing piece of music rather than, as she often does, a commissioned score, so she knew the music in some detail before choreographing with it. Nevertheless, she tends to avoid working too closely with the score while rehearsing, particularly in the earlier stages, because while the music is already complete in itself, the dance is still developing. As she says, she aims to make her choreography 'match' the strength of the music without 'mimicking' it.

➜ Volans, 'A Dialogue Between Collaborators', p. 15.

Although Volans had no direct input into the making of the piece, he did have two more general influences:

■ First, he introduced Davies and Buckland to the Shoowa designs.

Buckland referred to these in designing the floorcloth for *White Man Sleeps*; and both he and Davies were, like Volans, inspired by the balancing of order and chaos in the designs, and the human imprint and sense of evolution in the finished product. Since then, Davies has returned to these ideas frequently, most specifically in the making of *Bank* (1997).

▶ Designing White Man Sleeps, p. 52.

▶ Choreographic Developments, p. 22.

▶ A Dance in Time, p. 6.

■ The second idea that struck Davies was what Volans calls 'interlocking', a feature of much African music. At its simplest this involves a call-response structure, with the music alternating between different players. A more complex example is when two players have different rhythms which they play simultaneously, so that instead of being literally 'in time' with each other, they are 'interlocked' – independent and yet together. A further example is when different instrumentalists each play only one note at a time, and the musical theme only emerges when they play together. This idea can be seen in the instrumentation at the beginning of the score of *White Man Sleeps*:

© Chester Music Ltd. Reproduced by permission.

Instead of one instrument taking one part which the others accompany, or each instrument playing separate parts which are worked in counterpoint, here a single musical phrase is divided into two, a violin and cello alternating with the other violin and viola.

→ This can be seen in the opening sequence of the film, which shows the musicians playing this segment of the score; notice how the bows alternate.

Davies has referred to this concept in making choreography: distributing a rhythm or phrase between different dancers; or, on an individual

▶ Following the Work, pp. 88–9.

▶ White Man Sleeps Revisited, pp. 47–8.

● Task 4, p. 65.

▶ Dialogues in Dance, pp. 33–4.

➔ Volans, 'A Dialogue Between Collabora-tors', p. 15.

level, having different parts of the same body performing different rhythms or dynamics, so that the body works as an 'ensemble'. A simple example of the latter occurs in Lauren Potter's solo at the end of Part 3 of *White Man Sleeps*. The overall sense of this solo is of sinuous, fluid movement; but at two points, as she stretches into a long *arabesque* parallel with the floor, one arm suddenly flicks out to the side, seemingly independent from the rest of her. This division of the body echoes the two musical themes during this solo: one more melodic, a series of sustained, elongated coup-lets, the other a lightly plucked *pizzicato*. (In fact, Davies feels that she realised the idea of distributing rhythms and phrases more successfully in the reworked 1997 version of *White Man Sleeps* than in the original.)

It is also worth noting that in many ways 'interlocking' is a rich meta-phor for Davies's collaborative process, with the participants working both separately and in combination, and with the idea that the whole amounts to more than the sum of its parts. It also acts as a metaphor for the way the different strands of the dance – choreography, design, composition – inter-act together. As Davies has said, 'if we opened out the lattice work of both music and dance, allowing each to have the focus at different times . . . If the balance is right between the parts, then the sum will add up to more than first envisaged by choreographer and composer.'

Music/Dance Dialogue

'I try and think of the music as a *space* within which you move, in amongst the notes, rather than as a line where you go from note to note. It's a more three-dimensional environment. If you see a group of musicians working you get that sense much more than if you just listen. You see the music literally move amongst them – unlike with a score, where it appears very flat.' *Siobhan Davies*

Perhaps another way of putting this would be to say that, for Davies, the music and dance are 'interlocking'. This is different from the radical sepa-ration of music and dance that Cunningham developed; yet it is not dancing 'to' the music, or as a visualisation of it. For Davies, music and dance exist on different planes, and ideally, rather than one following the other, they create points of connection and congruence as well as separation, counterpoint or tension.

→ For a more detailed, technical account of musical-choreographic styles, see Jordan, *Moving Music*, Ch. 2.

On a broad level, the five-section form of *White Man Sleeps* echoes the five-movement form of the music; and in fact on a more detailed level, too, the dance tends to echo the musical changes of theme and phrase – for example, the 13-count phrases for the dancers in the opening part, which mirror the 13-count structure of the music. In Part 2 there is more variation of theme and dynamic in the music, and the dance again often corresponds to these changes fairly closely, shifting from the bright, bounding 'prairie runs', to a tender duet for Paul Douglas and Catherine Quinn, through to the more hushed solo interludes for Scott Clark.

▶ The Structure of the Dance, p. 73.

▶ Following the Work, pp. 84–7.

Davies admits that following musical cues so closely was partly a matter of expedience, given the short rehearsal period available; and certainly for the 1997 reworking of *White Man Sleeps* she developed more leeway between music and movement.

▶ White Man Sleeps Revisited, pp. 47–8.

Nevertheless, the musical cues followed are often its *changes* – which act as 'landmarks' in the musical environment through which the dance moves – and within these larger shifts of phrasing, theme and dynamic, there is considerable interplay between music and dance. (In fact, Kevin Volans, at the time a newcomer to watching dance, remembers that he 'didn't see how they were dancing to the music at all: it seemed quite perverse.') Certainly Davies prefers to develop dance phrases first, and only then find ways of fitting them alongside the music, so that within the broader cues of music the dance finds its own rhythms and dynamics.

● Task 5, p. 65.

→ Kimberley, 'Musical Collaborations', p. 32.

→ See Jordan, *striding Out*, pp. 152–4.

Some elements in *White Man Sleeps* showing the interplay between dance and music are:

■ Phrases performed in canon (a frequent device in Davies's works). In addition to their choreographic effects, a phrase performed in canon also has a particular rhythmic effect, setting up its own cross-rhythms between the dancers, and so complicating the relation of the phrase to the musical rhythm.

▶ Following the Work, p. 81.

■ Another choreographic device that Davies frequently uses, which also has musical effects, is to repeat different phrases or motifs at different points in the piece, when the music can be quite different. A clear example occurs in Part 4, Section C, during the 'travelling' ensemble sequence. Against the background travelling phrase, the dancers, either separately or in duets, perform many phrases of movement that have been introduced in earlier sections to different music, which are here adjusted in timing or dynamic in relation to the different metre of the music.

▶ Following the Work, p. 93.

▶ Film/Dance Dialogue, pp. 63–4.

■ Davies will often extend a dance phrase after the music has stopped, as occurs in Lauren Potter's solo which finishes Part 3 of *White Man Sleeps*. The effect is similar to a 'fade out': silence is reached before stillness. The dance seems to quieten, while the echoes of the last phrase of music reverberate in the memory.

▶ Following the Work, pp. 88–9.

■ In the 'fade out', stillness and silence overlap; they can also be contrasted (a device that Davies has used most strongly and deliberately in *Wild Air*, 1999). In the middle of Part 5 of *White Man Sleeps*, there is a relatively long freeze, with all the dancers holding the *animal head* motif; the music, meanwhile, continues its quiet thrumming. The effect here is to suggest anticipation, expectancy.

▶ Following the Work, p. 95.

▶ Key Motifs, p. 74.

■ The dancers' movements may or may not reflect the musical dynamics. In Part 2, the loping 'prairie runs' performed by Catherine Quinn and Paul Douglas mirror the timing and quality of the weightily bowed string instruments. But their duet that immediately follows is much slower and calmer, while the music continues to be strong and energetic. Then again, as the music quietens, their duet merges back into the music in becoming less spatially expansive and more intimate. The dance and music often merge and separate in this way.

▶ Following the Work, p. 84.

■ Davies often encourages her dancers to vary the phrasing and timing between fixed musical cues, as a way of keeping the performance 'alive', and also of finding different ways of relating to the music (a technique that

▶ Spatial Territories and New Music, p. 19.

▶ Dancers, p. 37.

can be deployed freely in solos, but not in duets or larger formations where the dancers need to co-ordinate their timings more closely).

▶ This could lead to problems in film editing. See Film/Dance Dialogue, p. 62.

White Man Sleeps Revisited

In 1997 Davies decided to revive *White Man Sleeps*, but instead of a straight-forward reconstruction, she reworked the piece considerably. Although all of the movement in the 1997 dance derived from the original version, it was often substantially transformed. On the one hand, revisiting the work allowed her to extend some of her original ideas, such as sharing a rhythm between different dancers, and it also gave her the opportunity to allow a more open interplay between music and dance rhythms and phrases. On the other hand, she also filtered some of her more recent movement concerns into the piece, adding more intricacy to the movement, for example by complicating some of the lifts, and aiming for a sharper dynamic edge.

▶ A Dance in Time, p. 8.

For the 1997 reworking, Davies chose to use Volans's original score for two harpsichords, viola da gamba and percussion, which gave a very different timbre to the music. Two reasons for this choice are:

■ In the 1988 version of *White Man Sleeps* Davies had explored fluid motion and 'liquid gesture'. In the intervening years, particularly after *Wild Translations* and *The Art of Touch* (both 1995), she had extended her dynamic range to include a sharper edge, and had developed the detail and complexity of body motion to produce a less 'unified' sense of movement, with different parts of the body taking up different rhythms or acting in counterpoint with each other. The string quartet version of Volans's score produces a more homogeneous, blended sound than the original instrumentation: the violin, viola and cello are all similar types of instrument, differing in register and pitch rather than in technique and timbre. The more sharply differentiated sounds of the harpsichords, viola da gamba and percussion therefore seemed more suited to her movement concerns in 1997.

→ Jordan, *Striding Out*, p. 143.

▶ Choreographic Developments, p. 17.

The 1997 version of *White Man Sleeps.* Paul Old, Gill Clarke, and Sean Feldman. Photo: Sean Hudson

▶ Dialogues in Dance, pp. 33–4.

▶ A Dance in Time, p. 8.

■ Two of the dancers from 1988 also performed in the 1997 piece: Catherine Quinn, who performed at the premiere, and Gill Clarke who took over the role on tour. Nevertheless, in accordance with her preferred process of collaboration and dialogue, Davies wanted *all* the dancers to contribute individually to the piece, rather than trying to duplicate previous movement made for different dancers. Choosing the different score made this process easier, creating a sense of distance from the 1988 dance. Furthermore, one movement of the music is completely different, for which Davies choreographed a new section of dance.

Design

The set and costume designer for *White Man Sleeps* was Davies's frequent collaborator, David Buckland, who has also worked with photography and film. The lighting was by Peter Mumford, another regular collaborator, who also directed the film of *White Man Sleeps*, shown on Channel 4 television in 1989.

▶ Film, pp. 55–64.

Designing for Dance

As Buckland points out, designing for dance, especially dance without an explicit narrative programme (as with *White Man Sleeps*), has very different requirements from designing for theatre or opera:

→ See also, Buckland, 'Design in Motion'.

■ *Space* is at a premium. There is relatively little that can be put onto the stage itself without overly impinging on the dancers' movement: singers and actors can much more easily adjust to or incorporate objects and props on the stage without it obstructing their medium of communication. The main areas for design for dance are generally (though not exclusively): the backdrop, the frontcloth, the floor (as in *White Man Sleeps*), the sides and the space above. One way of creating an onstage design for the dance without obstructing it is to use lighting effects, which allows freedom of motion at the same time as casting an atmosphere or creating a specific 'environment' for the dance. Of course, a set can be designed for the stage space itself – such as Buckland's moving metal grilles for Davies's *Wanting to Tell Stories* (1993) – but it needs to be carefully integrated into the choreography. Buckland recognises, too, that an overly heavy or busy design can overwhelm the intimate scale of the more detailed and subtle movements that Davies often uses.

▶ Lighting, pp. 52–4.

● Task 6, p. 65.

■ There is no *script* or *programme* to work to. A narrative idea and a cast of characters can act as a central reference point for designer, choreographer and composer to represent the action in the plot and differentiate the characters appropriately. A script also gives collaborators an idea of what to aim for in advance of seeing rehearsals for the production. Such a script is far more common in opera and theatre, where there is a text and/or a score. In dance, a plot or setting can also act as a reference point – but Davies very rarely follows such a programme, and she tends to evoke character and situation through the movements performed, rather than to represent them directly; and these allusions generally emerge and gain focus during the course of rehearsals, rather than in advance.

▶ Interpreting the Work, pp. 106–10.

■ Because Davies focuses much of her attention on qualities that emerge from the movement itself, costumes need to allow the dancers' move-ments to be seen clearly by the audience, and not to obstruct the freedom of movement required to perform the choreography. Often with Davies, the costumes for the dancers are relatively similar for all the dancers without being exactly the same. The costumes, then, allow the movement to speak for itself without overloading it with other meanings.

Designing White Man Sleeps

White Man Sleeps was made in about three weeks; Buckland first saw rehearsals about half way through this period. However, having been with Davies on their trip to America the previous year, and having worked with her on *Wyoming* on their return, he would already have known about many of the concerns that Davies was exploring at the time.

▶ An American Sabbatical, p. 15.

The Floorcloth

Two main factors can be seen to have influenced the floorcloth:

■ The idea of landscape. While in America, Davies had visited the plains

An example of a Shoowa textile design. Photo: Simon Gough.

of the Midwest, and been struck by the particular emotive quality of the human figure in an expansive, flat landscape. This was a strong theme in *Wyoming*, made immediately before *White Man Sleeps*. Both *Wyoming* and *White Man Sleeps* were also designed for Riverside Studios in London, a non-proscenium space where the stage area is very broad, with open wings and a very high ceiling. Though it was a stronger feature of *Wyoming*, this sense of space and territory was also integral to *White Man Sleeps*. The design is very simple and open: a floorcloth demarcating the dancing area. The dancers could be seen walking on and off it, and there were no other elements to the set, leaving the space above and around the floorcloth empty.

▶ Music, p. 40.
Musical Sources, p. 43.

■ Shoowa designs. The composer, Kevin Volans, introduced Buckland and Davies to the African textile designs that had been so important to his own artistic development. Buckland designed the floorcloth with these textiles in mind, synthesising ideas taken from different textiles. The floorcloth is marked at irregular intervals with a patchwork of striped squares in black and white, and, like the Shoowa designs, maintains a sense of formal geometry without becoming in any way mechanical. The floorcloth (in fact made of linoleum) was also painted with a grained texture to suggest the ribbing of a handwoven textile.

● Task 7, p. 65.

Costumes

The costumes echo the design elements in the floorcloth. They were made of a thick cotton-lycra mixture, with deep ribbing that suggest a woven texture, in broad bands of blue, black and grey. The leotard shape allows freedom of movement for the dancers and clarity of perception for the audience. The costumes are similar for all the dancers, all made from the same coloured bands, but individually varied. Like the floorcloth, then, this imparts an organic sense of pattern rather than a mechanical one, a sense of being *unified* without also being *uniform*. And like the choreo-graphy itself, it holds in balance the ideas of belonging together as a group and maintaining a separate individuality (a frequent theme in Davies's work, and also a feature of her collaboration process).

▶ Dialogues in Dance,
pp. 33–4.
▶ Interpreting the Work,
pp. 106–10.

Lighting

→ See also Mumford,
'The Language of Light.'

The lighting design for *White Man Sleeps* works in two layers:

■ Perhaps the most recognisable feature relates to the floorcloth. Some of the striped patchwork squares on the floorcloth are lit directly from above in shafts of vertical light, highlighting the white stripes. The effect is to give these stripes an inner glow, almost as if they were lit from within. By bringing out a feature of the set design, the lighting acts as a 'bridge' between a still set and a live performance.

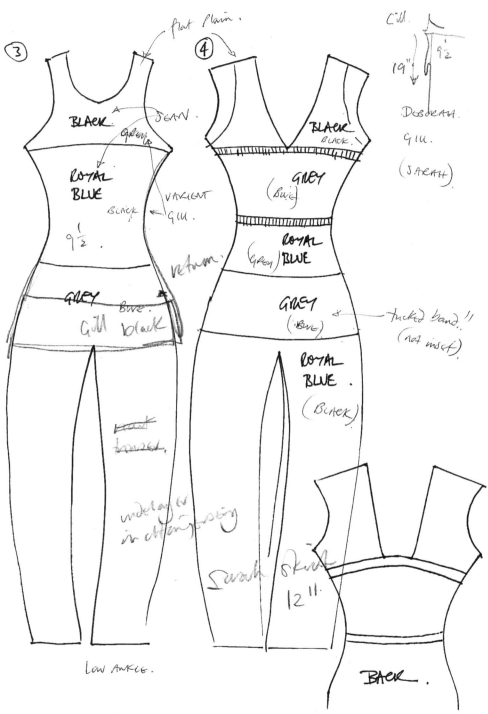

Working drawings by Sasha Keir for the remade costumes of the 1997 production of *White Man Sleeps*, after the original concept by David Buckland.

■ Though the dancers were lit by the vertical shafts of light as they passed through them, these toplights were not sufficient to show the dancers properly. Yet simply increasing the amount of light would destroy the effect of the floor lighting. Mumford's solution was to use sidelights focused off the floor, which lit the dancers without touching the floorcloth, thereby also separating the dancers' lighting from the 'environmental' lighting, increasing the focus on the dance by a contrast in lighting technique. In Michael Fulwell's solo that begins Part 3, only the sidelight is used, with no floor lighting, so that he seems almost suspended in the space.

▶ Following the Work, p. 88.

The lighting of *White Man Sleeps*, like the choreography itself, responds very much to musical cues and moods. The contrasts can be seen clearly, for example, in Part 2: the bouncy runs for Paul Douglas and Catherine Quinn, to strongly bowed music, are brightly lit; then, as the music quietens and thins for Scott Clark's solo interludes after the 'knocking' gesture, the lighting too dims dramatically. It was the music-led nature of both the lighting and choreographic cues that led Mumford to feature the musicians strongly in filming the piece.

▶ Following the Work, pp. 84–7.

▶ Film/Dance Dialogue, pp. 59–60.

White Man Sleeps Revisited

▶ White Man Sleeps Revisited, pp. 21–2. White Man Sleeps Revisited, pp. 47–8.

Unlike the music and the choreography, the designs for the 1997 reworking of *White Man Sleeps* remained essentially unchanged: the same floorcloth was used, and a similar lighting design. And though the costumes were remade for the dancers (by designer Sasha Keir), they replicated the original costumes as far as possible.

Film

White Man Sleeps was filmed for television by a small independent production company, Dance-Lines, which originated from a video workshop set up by Dance Umbrella at Riverside Studios, London, in 1986, with backing from Channel 4 and support from the Gulbenkian Foundation and the Digital Equipment Company. Led by Terry Braun and Peter Mumford, the idea behind the workshop was to allow an exchange of ideas, information and skills between choreographers, dancers and film-makers. This was to be an opportunity for choreographers and film-makers to learn each other's crafts, to explore ways of interacting, and to experiment with making dance for film and film for dance. The choreographers and dancers who participated included Ian Spink, Sally Owen, Paul Clayden, and Siobhan Davies, and the workshop was recorded in an hour-long documentary shown on Channel 4, entitled simply *Dance-Lines*.

The following year, the Dance-Lines team decided to commission choreographers to make a piece of dance for television, resulting in works by Richard Alston, Yolande Snaith and Ian Spink. Davies was in America on a Fulbright Fellowship that year, but on her return she collaborated again with Dance-Lines for their 1988 project. The results were *Wyoming* and *White Man Sleeps* (directed by Peter Mumford), filmed versions of the two stage works she created with her new company, broadcast on Channel 4 in 1989. *White Man Sleeps* went on to win an IMZ Dance Screen Award for best studio adaptation in 1991.

→ For more information on other Dance-Lines productions, see Rubidge, 'Recent Dance Made for Television', pp. 189–97, 200–4. See also de Marigny and Newman, 'Progressive Programming', and Penman, 'Ballet and Contemporary Dance on British Television'.

The works made by Dance-Lines in these projects were all made specially for film, rather than filmed versions of stage productions. This enabled more interaction between the film-makers, dancers and choreographers, and allowed the possibility of adapting (as with *Wyoming* and *White Man Sleeps*) or creating choreography specifically to be seen on film. Indeed, when making *Wyoming* and *White Man Sleeps* Davies already

→ For more on differences in filming techniques for studio and stage, see Lockyer 'Stage Dance on Television', and Nears 'Bridging a Distance'.

had the idea in mind that there would also be a film version. For *Wyoming*, this influenced the staged choreography considerably, but *White Man Sleeps* was less affected, partly because of the much shorter rehearsal period available. Nevertheless, Mumford had already worked closely with Davies in the first Dance-Lines project, and he had attended many rehearsals of both *Wyoming* and *White Man Sleeps* prior to their filming, as well as creating the lighting designs for both pieces, so he would have been very familiar with the themes of these works before starting on the studio filming.

Filming Dance

→ See also Lockyer 'Stage Dance on Television'; Nears, 'Bridging a Distance'.

There are many factors to take into account when filming dance, which affect what is seen and how it is seen. Some general points which constrain the translation of dance onto film are:

■ Film 'flattens' the three-dimensional perspective of the theatre, giving less feeling of depth to the space represented. Depth on film is often communicated more as an effect of *size* (whether the figure on screen is small or large) than of *distance* (whether the figure is near or far).

■ Film loses some of the physical and kinaesthetic immediacy of live dance: there is less sense of gravity, weight, exertion, momentum.

■ Perhaps the single most important feature of a filmed dance is that the camera necessarily selects what is shown. In the theatre, viewers will 'edit' what they see, shifting their gaze between different dancers, focusing on a group or an individual; but with filmed dance, that choice is made by the camera.

■ The frame of the screen defines the field of view. On television, this is a very small area, so the sense of space is restricted. A full figure will often appear very small on screen and a longer shot of a group may make the figures even smaller, losing both the detail and clarity of movement. On the other hand, a close-up shot cuts out parts of the dancer's body, and any other dancers or events outside its frame. While a close-up can often convey physicality more directly, it is less suitable for showing an overall design to the movement.

■ It is harder for dancers to do repeated 'takes' than for actors. A repeated action tires the muscles quickly. Furthermore, it is harder to do very short takes: in order to perform the movement fully, the dancers usually need a lead up, starting from the beginning of a phrase, and also a follow-through to complete the impulse of the movement.

■ Whereas on stage each performance of the piece will be slightly different, a filmed dance will be the same every time.

There are also techniques and effects that film can create which cannot be done on stage, such as:

■ Editing. A film can cut or dissolve from one shot to another, for example to show the same movement in both close-up and long-shot. The cuts, however, need not be connected by any physical or temporal logic.

■ There are numerous effects available on film, ranging from super-imposed images, through slow-motion and freeze effects to animation and visual filters.

■ The camera can range from very distant shots to extreme close-up, taking the viewer right into the stage space and amongst the dancers. Alternatively, it can create low- or high-angle shots, top shots, tracking shots, zooms in or out. Though the camera is more selective than the theatre viewer, it is also more mobile.

● Task 8, pp. 65–6.

■ Each camera acts as its own 'front', and this is moveable: the work need not be seen from a single front, as on a proscenium stage.

It is also worth noting the very different viewing contexts for staged and screened works. In a theatre, the audience is in a sense 'captive': once in their seats, it is relatively difficult for them to leave or enter during the course of a piece, whereas the television viewer can do this easily. The theatre audience also shares the same physical, public environment, whereas for a television audience this will vary widely. The television audience is also likely to be far more numerous and varied than the theatre audience.

→ See also Lockyer 'Stage Dance on Television', pp. 131–2.

Filming White Man Sleeps

→ See also Jordan, 'The Collaborations *White Man Sleeps* and *Wyoming*'; Somerville, 'A Contemporary Trio', pp. 83–5.

Mumford felt that too often dance was filmed voyeuristically, as if it were simply a matter of spectatorship rather than communication, and with *White Man Sleeps* he was concerned to find ways of translating the communicative language of the dance – its ideas, physical sensations, mood – into the medium of film. Hence he tended to avoid exclusively filmic devices which would radically *transform* rather than translate the dance (such as animation or image distortion, cuts without a physical or temporal logic), and focused on the creative use of the interface between dance and film. Nevertheless, he realised that there were gaps between the two media, and that the film medium would place constraints on the dance as well as opening up its own possibilities. The process could be likened to a shifting dialogue between film and dance, which contribute to the outcome both independently and in combination.

▶ Dialogues in Dance, pp. 33–4.

Film Tracks

The studio set for *White Man Sleeps* was roughly square in shape, rather than the longer rectangular shape of the stage. A cyc was placed along one wall, and the adjacent wall was used to project a film of the musician. Along the other two walls a track was built for a camera to move along. There were three basic types of camera shot used:

■ The tracking camera. This was set at mid-height and mounted on the track. The camera could swivel around a fixed point, zoom in or out, and also move along a horizontal plane defined by the track running around two sides of the studio. This camera was used for long shots, and could also zoom in to medium shot.

■ The hand-held camera. This was operated by cameraman Tony Keene, who could move in amongst the dancers. In order to do this, his movements had to be carefully choreographed into the dance so that he could view the piece without getting in the way of the dancers. The hand-held camera could move from long shot into extreme close-up. In *White Man Sleeps*, the hand-held shots were mainly done from mid-height, making cutting into shots made by the tracking camera more easy.

→ Compare this with the wider range of movement in the virtuoso opening sequence of *Wyoming*, a 13-minute single take by the hand-held camera.

■ The high-angle camera. This fixed-position camera at one side of the studio could swivel from this fixed point, and zoom in or out. This camera produced a high long-shot with a deeper perspective than the tracking camera.

In addition to filming the dance, there was a second film track of the musicians playing, taken almost entirely in close-up (apart from some clips in the last part), and filmed in black and white rather than colour.

Lastly, there was the sound track of the musicians playing, synchronised with both the dance and music visual tracks.

Film/Dance Dialogue

■ Perhaps the most striking difference between the film and stage versions is the presence of the musicians. At Riverside Studios, the quartet was placed to one side, but on film they have a much stronger visual presence. The visual track of the musicians playing is related to the dance track in a number of different ways. Clips of the musicians begin and end

► Following the Work, p. 79.

the film, and are spliced between and sometimes within the five parts; there are also occasional shots of the musicians superimposed upon the dancers. This visual track also appears *within* the dance track: during the piece, the film of the musicians was projected onto the back wall of the studio, and occasionally also onto the floor. These separate filmic layers can be seen in sequence at the beginning of the film: the clip of the musicians playing dissolves almost imperceptibly into the same clip projected onto the back wall, so that when the first dancer (Paul Douglas) enters, he appears almost to arise out of the music. The score is much more visually present throughout the film than it had been on stage, and this visual track is contrasted with the dance in both scale (the close-up shots make the musicians loom much larger than the dancers) and colour (black-and-white against colour). The music thus provides a visual as well as an aural 'environment' for the dance to move through.

▶ Music/Dance Dialogue, p. 44.

■ *White Man Sleeps* lent itself to filming because there was often a clear focus to the action on stage, so the camera could select its frame relatively easily. This is much more difficult to do when there is a divided focus, with different actions happening simultaneously in different places. Where this did occur, different techniques could be used. For example, when the dancers are more spread across the stage, the high-angle shot was sometimes used to keep them all in frame. Or, towards the end of the Part 1, where two lines of dancers are placed at opposite sides of the stage, the film frame repositioned them as foreground and background rather than left and right, keeping both lines in frame while still suggesting the width between them as an effect of size rather than distance.

▶ A Dance in Time, p. 6.
▶ Following the Work, p. 81.

■ In the choreography, Davies emphasised seamless, flowing movement and 'liquid' gesture. This quality is reflected in the cuts, which are unobtrusive, without 'jump' cuts, and often follow musical or movement cues. It is also found in much of the camerawork, which is very mobile. The tracking camera almost always follows the line of movement of the dancers; even more so, the hand-held camera could move fluidly in congruence with the movement. Spiralling motion was a particular feature of the choreography, and the hand-held camera was able to follow Scott Clark's spiral to the floor in his opening solo in Part 4, or Lauren Potter's spiral up from the floor in her duet with Michael Fulwell in Section B of Part 2, or the spiralling lifts in the duets for Quinn and Douglas earlier in the same section. Perhaps the confluence of camera and dancer is best seen in Potter's solo which closes Part 3, recorded in a single take by the hand-held camera. Keeping Potter mainly in full frame, the camera here is remarkably mobile, so that the space around Potter, and between her and the camera, seems to become almost as sinuously mobile as Potter herself.

▶ Following the Work, p. 91.

▶ Following the Work, p. 87.

▶ Following the Work, pp. 84–7.

▶ Following the Work, p. 88–9.

■ Different qualities of the same movement can be brought out by cutting, as a way of expanding the selectiveness of the camera frame. So a phrase can be cut from long shot, which shows the shape of the movement, into close-up, which brings out its physicality. This is a frequent device in the filming.

■ Occasionally cutting was used to play filmic tricks. Examples are the dissolve which ends Michael Fulwell's solo that begins Part 3, so that Paul Douglas and Scott Clark seem suddenly to 'appear' in mid-stage next to him; or the cut towards the end of Scott Clark's solo opening Section 4 which enabled the sudden 'appearance' of Lauren Potter in the foreground.

▶ Following the Work, p. 88.

▶ Following the Work, p. 91.

■ Part 5 was the most complex to shoot in spatial terms, because it used much of the ensemble on stage simultaneously in different places, particularly in the middle section, where phrases of movement ending in the *animal head* motif are passed between different dancers, who enter and exit at different times. This section of the film contains the most cutting, between the tracking camera and the high-angle camera. The rapid cutting between angles adds its own edgy dynamic to the interplay of movement; significantly, in this section some fragments of *reverse tracking* – where the camera moves in the opposite direction to the line of movement – were also used, increasing the dynamic tension of this section of dance.

▶ Key Motifs, p. 74.

▶ Following the Work, p. 95.

■ The high-angle shot was used as a way of heightening perspective and distance, which often appears flattened from a mid-height camera. From the high angle the dancers appear to advance and recede much more noticeably, and to cover more space. The shot also encompasses the whole studio area, allowing a widely separated group of dancers to be kept in frame. It also enabled the dancers to enter and exit the screen frame in different directions from the usual left or right required by the stage or by the mid-height tracking camera, using the top and bottom of the screen, for example, or exiting across a diagonal, giving a more 'open' feel to the framing.

▶ Designing White Man Sleeps, p. 51.

■ Mumford had not realised that although Davies often coincides dance cues with musical ones, between these cues she encourages dancers to 'play' within the phrase, so that they don't perform the phrase in the same way each time (a feature of her own performances as a dancer). This made cutting together film from different *takes* an occasional problem: the dancers were in different positions on the different takes, making it hard to splice the film together seamlessly. On the final film, clearly, these variations of live performance are lost.

▶ Music/Dance Dialogue, pp. 46–7.

■ As in many of Davies's dances, phrases are repeated at different angles and orientations, allowing the viewer to register movements without relying on direct repetition. The camera could easily work in the same way, giving the viewer a different angle on the same phrase during its repeats. It could also *add* its own perspectives, from the high-angle camera, or from the hand-held camera. The close-up shots, particularly, were able to communicate a different physical sensation and to magnify small movements in a different way from in the theatre. There are many instances where a gentle intimacy of touch is brought out by the hand-held camera. For example, in the duets for Catherine Quinn and Paul Douglas in Part 2, the camera could focus on the sensual quality of touch and weight. Later in the same duet, it placed Quinn's small, delicate knocking against Douglas's shoulder in the extreme foreground, so that when Scott Clark appeared in the background, the effect was almost as if Quinn's gentle knocking had opened a distant, unseen door from which Clark emerged.

▶ Following the Work, pp. 84–7.

The final part of the piece. Left to right: Paul Douglas, Catherine Quinn, Lauren Potter, Michael Fulwell. Photo: David Buckland

■ Occasionally the choreography needed to be changed for the camera in order to convey a similar idea to the stage effect. Sometimes this involved simply shifting 'front' to face the tracking or high-angle camera. But the most significant change occurred in Part 4, Section C: the 'travelling' sequence in which the ensemble journeys together in a simple repeated phrase. In the stage version, the travelling phrase moved around the edges of the stage. As Mumford noted, however, the important *idea* was of continuous travel rather than moving around a perimeter; he felt that the dancers circled the stage simply because there was nowhere else to go. Circling would have produced a very different effect on film, with its small frame and lack of depth. Instead, the sequence was filmed in several takes and performed in one direction only, and through repeatedly cutting the

▶ Following the Work, pp. 91–3.

▶ A Dance in Time, p. 5.

dancers as they crossed the screen, Mumford was able to suggest the idea of continuous travel from right to left.

▶ Following the Work, p. 53.

▶ A Dance in Time, p. 6.

■ Sometimes the principal idea behind the movement was not translatable onto screen. In Scott Clark's solo which opens Part 4, for example, the idea had been to contrast a lone figure against a large space, his extended arms suggesting the length and dimensions of that space. On film, it was felt that the long shot required to encompass the space would produce too small a figure for this to work effectively. Instead this was filmed with a hand-held camera in close-up, which brought out a different quality to the movement: the idea of space recedes, and the solo now conveys a more intimate, sensual impression as he traces the line of his arm, or the shape of the spiral as he moves to the floor.

● Task 9, p. 66.

Lyric Television

▶ Dialogues in Dance, pp. 33–4.

→ Jordan, 'The Collaborations *White Mans Sleeps* and *Wyoming*', p. 182.

▶ Interpreting the Work, pp. 105–6.

In many films and television programmes, the various techniques of framing, shooting and cutting are organised to express a central (often narrative) idea, to transmit a particular message to the viewer. Davies's choreography rarely operates in this way: she prefers to communicate by focusing on the medium, and allowing messages to be generated in dialogue between its different strands of dance, music, and design, and in dialogue with the viewers. Accordingly, in filming *White Man Sleeps*, Mumford was aiming to create 'a kind of lyric television', more poetic than narrative in style, in which the filming techniques are deployed more freely to convey the qualities of the medium rather than to express a particular message. Instead of acting as a receptor of information, the viewer is asked to engage imaginatively with the film as a participant. The film of *White Man Sleeps*, like the work on which it is based, thus echoes the collaborative, dialogic nature of both the form of the piece and the process of its creation.

Tasks

1. Choose a small section of *White Man Sleeps* and look at the various strands – dancers, music, design. Identify moments which illustrate different ways that they relate to each other: overlaps, congruence, antagonism, independence, dominance? What effects do these produce?

2. Group discussion. (a) Take a short section of *White Man Sleeps* and write down a list of images and associations that you respond to. Compare your answers with other people's. How are the answers similar or different? Why do you think that might be? (b) Compare ways in which you might look at *White Man Sleeps* with how you could look at, for example, a work by Merce Cunningham, or a narrative ballet, or another dance of your own choice. What is it about these dances that suggest particular ways of seeing?

3. Improvise with animal imagery. Start with just one part of the body, and imagine that it is part of a particular animal. Then choose another part of the body, and a different animal. Now try putting the movements together, and keeping the feeling of each animal in the different parts. How does the movement feel? How does it look?

4. Working with a partner, each make one short phrase of movement, based on a particular rhythm. Set the two phrases next to each other and experiment with the different ways that their timings can 'interlock', by starting at different times, or varying their speed. Then, with each phrase in turn, explore how one phrase can be divided up into a duet, so that one original phrase is now shared between two people.

5. Choose a section of music, and with the phrase made in (4) above, explore how the rhythm can 'interlock' with the music, coinciding at cue points and varying in between. Combine your phrases to the music in a short compositional study that illustrates different ways the phrases relate to each other and to the music.

6. Look at the set, costume and lighting design for different dances. Describe the design, and the subject and style of the choreography. How does the choreography interact with the design elements? How is the design appropriate to the theme?

7. Using a design or textile of your choice, write down what you consider its main features: is it geometrical, organic, changeable, bold, subtle, textured, plain? Starting from a movement phrase that you have already made, see if you can develop it by incorporating some of the ideas from the design.

8. If you have video equipment available, experiment with filming a piece of dance. Try filming a moving dancer from a fixed position. Then try filming a stationary dancer with a moving camera. What do you learn about the film/dance relation? Experiment with different distances, angles and framings. If you have editing facilities, experiment with cutting between these shots. What are the effects produced for

each shot? Are they appropriate to the subject? How does the camera affect what is seen by the viewer?

9. Take a very short segment of the film which includes a clip of the musicians playing. (a) Focusing on the dance track only, identify how many cuts there are, and whether they are straight cuts or dissolves. Then identify the types of shot in the sequence: which camera is being used – the high-angle, the tracking camera, or the hand-held camera? Is the camera moving or fixed? What is seen in the frame? At what points does the editing of the sequence show continuities or changes in the choreography? (b) Now look at the track of the musicians playing. Is it spliced into the dance track or superimposed? Does this coincide with movement cues, cuts or different camera shots in the dance track? (c) Now listen to the soundtrack. Does the editing of the visual tracks identified above coincide with musical cues? Write a description of the film segment, and relate its impressions to the techniques of framing, shooting and editing that you have discovered.

Part 4

Contents

Sarah Whatley

An analysis of the choreographic content of White Man Sleeps

Rehearsal picture of Paul Douglas,
Catherine Quinn and Scott Clark in
the opening sequence of the dance.
(Part 1, Section A.)
Photo: David Buckland

Elements of the Work

In some important ways, *White Man Sleeps* clarifies and emphasises choreographic concerns that were evident in Davies's work prior to 1988; but here they are much more clearly articulated. The dance includes a number of elements which can also be identified in works choreographed since 1988, and thus can be said to have formed a basis or foundation for her choreographic style from that point on. These elements, which recur both within this dance and in later works, contribute to distinguishing Davies's movement vocabulary from that of her contemporaries. As in many of her works, the collaboration between Davies and her dancers, the music and design is one of the most important aspects of *White Man Sleeps*. The dance is developed through a networking of ideas, a careful and balanced sharing of the creative vision, without either losing the integrity of each collaborator or imposing a single authority on the work.

▶ Dialogues in Dance, pp. 33–4.

The Dancers

Prior to forming her own company in 1988, Davies was unable to give as much rehearsal time as she would have liked to exploring and investigating movement vocabulary. The dancers she gathered to work with in 1988 were all keen to engage in this exploration with her, to reassess their own knowledge and technique. *White Man Sleeps* is choreographed for five dancers; in the film they are Scott Clark, Paul Douglas, Michael Fulwell, Lauren Potter and Catherine Quinn. Paul Douglas and Lauren Potter were experienced, mature dancers who had worked with Davies before with London Contemporary Dance Theatre. Michael Fulwell was completing his training at London Contemporary Dance School when Davies invited him to work with her. Initially, Lizie Saunderson, who had worked with Davies

▶ Dancers, pp. 35–9.

in Second Stride, was dancing, but an injury just days before the opening meant she could not perform. Catherine Quinn, an Australian dancer, was in the country waiting to join Rambert Dance Company, and Davies asked her to step in and learn the role. Gill Clarke performed the work for the summer tour the following year, replacing Quinn who had started work with Rambert Dance Company. Finally, Davies asked Scott Clark to join the company. Clark's 'role' or 'character' in the dance is highly individualistic as it colours and weaves a thread through the dance. Many of these dancers have had a long association with the company.

▶ Dancers, p. 38.

Since 1988, Davies's relationship with her dancers has been central to the way her work has developed. Her choreographic process has encouraged the dancers to play and experiment with movement ideas and tasks given by her; they frequently contribute their own material and find their own movement solutions. This way of working has enabled the dancers to be active collaborators and decision-makers in the work, which communicates a sense of 'community' in each performance, while also emphasising each dancer's individual qualities.

▶ Dancers, pp. 35–9.

● Task 1, p. 96.

Music

The title *White Man Sleeps* comes from the music of the same name composed by Kevin Volans in 1982. Volans was born and brought up in South Africa and there are clear references to his African roots in the music. The music was originally composed for harpsichords, viola da gamba and percussion. *White Man Sleeps* was choreographed to the re-worked 1986 version for string quartet, but when the piece was revived in 1997 Davies returned to the original scoring.

▶ Music, pp. 40–8.

Design

The design for *White Man Sleeps* includes a floorcloth, costumes and lighting. All these aspects combine to communicate moods, images and textures which are present in the music and movement. Lighting states suggest different times of the day, an environment where the inhabitants are more 'in touch' with the elements, and are a community, working collectively.

▶ Design, pp. 49–54.

Film

The filming plays a critical role in the audience's perception of the dance. There are different camera angles, varying the distance and proximity to the dancing bodies, and the black-and-white film of the musicians is layered both behind and within the dance action. However, as the detail of the dance material is clear for much of the time, it is possible to describe the action, the way dancers interact with each other, the relationship of the movement to the music and the dynamic content, although the perception of all of these aspects and any interpretations of the movement material are, to some extent, guided or suggested by the camera.

▶ Film, pp. 55–64.

Introducing the Work

Source Material and Thematic Content

▶ Music, pp. 40–2.

▶ Music, p. 41.

The choreography sensitively and perceptively reflects the African-influenced rhythms, layering of sound and musical phrasing. Inferences to something tribal and ritualistic suggest Davies was responding both to the music and her experience in America of various aspects of Native American culture. The title itself is rich with possible interpretations: the idea of something quiet, private or unseen, of activity taking place away from the main action. Although Davies's experiences in America may have provided her with images and ideas which informed her movement exploration, the dancers were not necessarily given this imagery to generate movement, but rather it was used by Davies to clarify action, and to edit and shape the dancers' material. In this way, it can be said that the imagery gives the movement resonance and can suggest meaning, but the subject matter is primarily communicated through the movement itself rather than following a narrative or telling one story.

Movement

diversifying movement through experimentation

▶ Dancers, p. 37.

Throughout the dance, movement is repeated many times and shared between different dancers, although movement is frequently altered in some way, to face a new front, or reordered, danced in canon or changed in speed. Shapes created by the body are not held for long: they are fleeting, momentary and rarely borrowed from or based on any codified movement technique or vocabulary. Those elements of other vocabularies which can be identified from time to time are changed or altered, thereby making familiar movements strange, unusual and unpredictable.

The dancers move purposely across and around the edges of the space as if marking out their territory and establishing their place in the world.

▶ A Dance in Time, pp. 5–6.

As in many of Davies's works, both prior to and since 1988, the duet form recurs throughout the dance. Touch is functional, but considerate, less about developing a narrative between two dancers or characters, more about the way the human body responds to giving and sharing weight. Some partnering work suggests Davies developed the material from contact improvisation. Several duets in works choreographed by Davies since 1988 also appear to have developed in this way, including a duet for Paul Douglas and Amanda Britton in *Wild Translations* (1995), and material for Sarah Warsop and Henry Montes in *Eighty Eight* (1998).

→ On contact improvisation see Novack, *Sharing the Dance*; Mackrell, *Out of Line*.

The Structure of the Dance

Revising structure to keep image fresh?

The dance reflects the structure of the music, which is subdivided into five different 'dances'. It can therefore be said that *White Man Sleeps* is subdivided into five clear parts, linked in each case by film of the musicians. Although the dance makes a seamless whole, each part brings a mood change determined partly by the music, reinforced by lighting, the grouping of dancers, and dynamic and spatial content of the dance material.

▶ Music/Dance Dialogue, p. 45.

Parts can be further divided into sections, determined by changes in number of dancers or other performance aspects.

Key Motifs

The richly complex and fluid movement material means that body designs emerge only infrequently in the choreography. However, a number of *key motifs* recur, either repeated identically or developed in some way, and can be said to be important in giving the dance identity. Some are referred to in the detailed analysis in 'Following the Work' (pp. 79–95), so are described here for ease of reference:

▶ A Note on Labanotation, p. 98i.

■ *Animal head*. The body is in profile, the hands meet horizontally, outstretched with soft elbow joints, in front of the face with palms together. Although this gesture is seen throughout the dance and often marks a stillness or end of phrase, it does not appear to signify or represent any one thing, although the relationship of the hands to the face could be interpreted as the dancer tracing the shape of the muzzle of an animal, or the beak of a bird. It could also be interpreted as a concluding gesture, a return to stillness before moving off again, or simply as a shared gesture between the community of dancers. The name of this motif came after a conversation with Gill Clarke, who seemed to remember that Davies took the shape from an idea from one of her children.

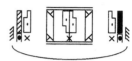

■ *Tailbone-back*. This movement is seen many times. After the dancer walks on stage in a neutral, natural manner at the start of the dance, it begins the opening movement phrase. It is also seen as an opening movement in later phrases. The movement is seen in profile, the dancer directs the tailbones or 'sitbones' (ischial tuberosities) backwards, dropping into weighty legs with movement directed towards the back leg, allowing one leg to stretch along the floor in front of the body, foot flat on the floor, while the other leg bends underneath to take the weight. The head reaches upwards and forwards, the back lengthens, bringing about an extension or counterpull between the top of the head and the pelvis. It is a transitional move, always leading directly into more movement.

■ *Tomahawk*. One arm swings high and forward, hinging from the elbow, taking the focus high, while the opposite leg swings high and backwards, hinging from the knee. There is a counterpull between the hinge joints of the elbow and knee. The shape of the body is suggestive of wielding/displaying a tomahawk, in a spiritual or ritual context. This movement is seen throughout the dance although it varies in size and speed, sometimes increasing the depth of the swing in the arm and body from a low level into the final shape. It is a transitional move, always leading directly into more movement.

■ *Shoulder shake*. Soft shoulder shakes, taking the body over forwards towards the floor. This idea of shaking out the arms, as if releasing tension in the shoulders and torso, and emphasising the jointed quality of the limbs, recurs in many different, moderated forms throughout Davies's work since 1988, for example in *White Bird Featherless* (1992), and *The Art of Touch* (1995).

■ *Sky and earth*. A fast, travelling step which skims the floor, often preceding fast footwork, propelling the dancer through space. The body alternates from looking up with arms reaching upwards, the back gently arching as the dancer hops forwards, to looking down, continuing the hops, with the back curving forwards, suggesting looking to sky and earth. The movement is performed in circular pathways, giving a tribal, or ritualistic feeling to this movement.

● Notation Task 1, p. 99.
Notation Task 2, p. 99.

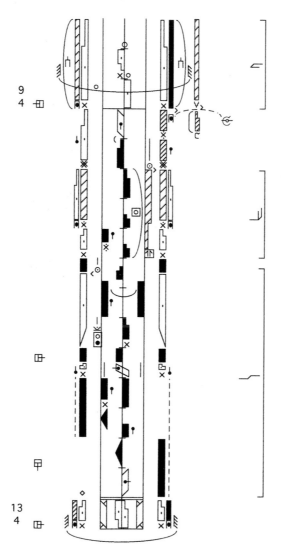

■ *Framing face*. The hands and arms frame the face with the elbows soft. This is performed by solo dancers and is suggestive of comforting self, or holding self together. The idea is developed in duets where hands and arms frame, or trace the outline of the head or face of another. (Note: although the *animal head* and *framing face* motifs are identified separately here, the organic nature of the movement development may mean that the *framing face* motif emerged through the way in which the *animal head* motif was transformed and developed through the dance.)

■ *Counterpull attitude*. There is a sense of counterpull between the arms and the back leg in *attitude* position, in a movement that has recurred in many of Davies's works, both prior to and since 1988. The movement occurs in several variations, sometimes close to the Cunningham-style tilted *attitude* (the body tilted over the supporting leg, parallel to the floor, and the arms in a vertical line) sometimes softer and more upright (as in this illustration). The movement is repeated many times in different ways – danced alone, in duets, and sometimes supported by another. It is rarely held for any length of time, and is suspended, or hovers in space, often with the body falling forwards, suggesting continual movement, and emphasising counterpull or the distance between body parts.

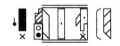

● Task 2, p. 96.

The key characteristics of the dance are summarised in the table overleaf. A more detailed analysis of the dance is then given in the following sections (pp. 79–95).

Key Characteristics of the Dance

Key
Motifs

- animal head
- tailbone–back
- tomahawk
- shoulder shake
- sky and earth
- framing face
- counterpull attitude

Action
Content

- emphasis on passage of movement through the body, not on end positions or body shapes
- subverting/diverting movement before completed – the resolution of one movement becomes the beginning of another
- relaxed, neutral body posture, musculature and performance manner
- gestural, in particular arm gestures
- sequential, successive flow of movement through the body, centrally initiated (often beginning in the pelvis)
- full range of articulations of the spine: curves, arches and twists
- low elevation, skimming, darting, skidding across the floor, fast weight changes
- travelling
- limb extensions to emphasise distance and movement between extremities, not body designs
- suspension, balance to off-balance
- flexion in ankles, knees, pelvis and elbows – jointed, but not angular
- floorwork, giving stability
- turning, spiralling
- partnering work and 'limb tracing'
- same material repeated with slight variations and embellishments, adding gestures or whole body movements, or turned around in space

Dynamic
Content

- use of both breath rhythm and musical rhythm to determine phrasing
- different speeds, varying energy levels but predominantly lilting, soft, swinging and rebounding
- fluid, rippling, lightly punctuated and accented – pauses and brief stillness then flurries of activity reflecting the interplay between musical instruments and contrast between the different sound of the strings (bowed or plucked)
- same material repeated with different quality or rhythm, or set to different music – so looks fresh

Spatial
Content

- spatial progression emphasised, body shape/body design de-emphasised
- travelling across the stage space, from right to left and back again
- travelling around the edges of the space
- circular pathways
- unprojected focus, rarely extended beyond own kinesphere
- repetition and transformation of movement with different spatial orientation/facing new fronts/changing levels/changing direction

Thematic
Content

- travelling, sense of distance, making a journey
- tribal, ritualistic, non-Western, Native American
- connecting or relating to a natural environment, to sky, earth, light and dark
- sense of community, common purpose, intimacy, separation, individuality, co-operation and collectivity

Following the Work

Part 1

The dance film begins with the musicians playing. At once, the close proximity of the camera to their playing draws attention to the movement of the bows on the strings, the complexity of the rhythms and layering of sounds.

▶ Film/Dance Dialogue, p. 59.

▶ Musical Sources, p. 43.

Section A

Paul Douglas enters, walking in a circle before beginning a fluid, seamless phrase of material which is transformed and made reference to in many different ways throughout the dance. One by one the other dancers join in, and the slippery, watery dynamic continues, the movement meandering comfortably through their bodies as they glide effortlessly across the stage and back again. The clarity of this opening material, repeated in unison and in straightforward canons across the stage, establishes the idea of travel, of distance, of making a journey, and indicates the way much of the movement is shared and organised throughout the dance. The opening material introduces the *animal head* motif, which is seen many times, drawing the dancers to stillness and punctuating the travelling phrase. It also includes the *tomahawk* and *shoulder shake* motifs. The frequent repetition of dance phrases mirrors the way the musical phrase is repeated many times.

▶ Key Motifs, p. 74.

▶ Key Motifs, p. 75.

Section B

Michael Fulwell enters, dancing the same phrase, and is closely followed by Lauren Potter, who introduces a new, faster travelling phrase, which

Lauren Potter and Michael
Fulwell (Part 1, Section B).
Photo: David Buckland

includes the *sky and earth* motif. As the music quietens, Fulwell and Potter meet and move together, joining and parting, clearly making eye contact, with easy lifts, careful supports and balances, leading to brief moments of rest. These more private, intimate moments give way to faster, more elevated material as the music returns to the more insistent, driven quality, which propels the two dancers on again, repeating the *sky and earth* motif. Fulwell briefly traces his hands around Potter's face. This introduces the *framing face* motif for the first time.

▶ Key Motifs, p. 76.

▶ Key Motifs, p. 77.

Section C

The other dancers return, circling the stage and accentuating the sense of travel. The group now re-forms downstage, and as the density of the music increases the opening movement phrase is danced in canon, changing fronts, yet moving much less across the space. The gentle, easy dynamic continues. This is a familiar device used by Davies in many of her works: a group of dancers is assembled closely together and a movement phrase or combination of phrases is performed in various canons, with pauses and directional or spatial changes. In this way, a small amount of movement material can be made complex by sharing it in a variety of ways between a group.

One by one, three of the dancers break off into repeating the travelling pattern across the stage, which includes the *sky and earth* motif, before a repeat of the canon material in a group, stage left. The part concludes with Fulwell and Potter dancing a variation of moments from earlier material. This short duet comes to rest in a version of the *counterpull attitude* motif, the man supporting the woman.

● Task 3, p. 96.

▶ Key Motifs, p. 76.

▶ Key Motifs, p. 77.

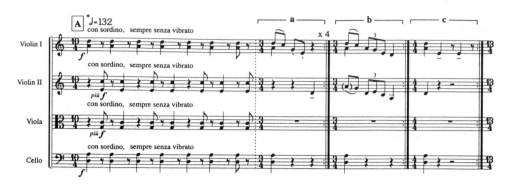

The opening of the First Dance in Volans's score.

© Chester Music Ltd. Reproduced by permission.

Part 1: A Summary

	Section A trio (Douglas, Quinn, Clark) canon/unison	Section B duet (Potter, Fulwell)	Section C group canon/unison
Key Motifs	• animal head • tailbone–back • tomahawk • shoulder shake	• animal head • tailbone–back • tomahawk • shoulder shake • sky and earth • framing face • counterpull attitude	• animal head • tailbone–back • tomahawk • shoulder shake • sky and earth • counterpull attitude
Action Content	• gestures • low elevation, skimming the floor • travelling • centrally initiated/torso initiated pathways within the body • quick succession of body parts/highly articulate • neutral body alignment and relaxed body attitude	• as Section A, plus: • faster travelling • partnering (lifts, balances)	• As Section A, plus: • faster travelling • partnering (lifts, balances)
Dynamic Content	• swing • rebound • fluid, continuous	• swing • rebound • fluid, continuous	• swing • rebound • fluid, continuous
Spatial Content	• circular pathways • travelling across the stage • unprojected focus • little body design	• circular pathways • travelling across the stage • unprojected focus • little body design	• circular pathways • travelling across the stage • unprojected focus • little body design • group 'clump'
Thematic Content	• introducing sense of travel/distance/making a journey • tribal, ritualistic non-western, native American • connection to natural elements; sky and earth • a community (about people) • activity to stillness	• as Section A, plus: • travel and distance with rest/pause for contact between male/female	• As Section A

Part 2

This is a complex part, and can be subdivided into two distinct sections. There are a number of clear changes in the music throughout this part, most notably when the second section begins, and for the final duet when the music becomes triplets in 4/2 time.

Section A

(a) The couple that concluded Part 1 (Fulwell and Potter) begins the first section of Part 2, with faster, more spirited, energetic material. Some familiar material returns, but there is more tension, more counterpull between the diagonals, and less time to suspend the movement. The music drives the dancers on as they cover more space, swept across the stage and back again.

(b) The focus switches to Catherine Quinn, who dances a solo – a short phrase of movement repeated three times, facing the right diagonal front, the left diagonal front, then the right diagonal once more. The *framing face* ▶ Key Motifs, p. 7. motif recurs, punctuating the phrase. She continues the feeling of being swept as she throws her limbs away to the side of her body, releasing energy right through to the extremities of her feet and hands, following breath rhythm, relaxed, yet with clarity and direction. She ends kneeling on one knee, at rest, as the music slows.

(c) A dramatic change in both music and lights brings on Scott Clark, who moves downstage with a brief solo – a series of loose twists and spirals – while Quinn continues with slow solo material and the first couple perform a slow and sustained duet upstage.

(a1) The music begins to speed again and the couple perform the circular travelling pattern, which includes the *sky and earth* motif, concluding with ▶ Key Motifs, p. 76. material from the duet at the start of this section, before making a fast exit, running off stage together.

Section B

Throughout this section, which includes a lot of new material, we see a bold, running step, circling the stage, performed by Paul Douglas and Catherine Quinn. Extended natural runs, they emphasise a sense of energy and a confidence in travelling through space. The runs suggest the dancers are covering a large expanse of ground. They seem to be running after each other, playfully, to catch up, or overtake. The runs always result in a lift, the man lifting the woman high above him in a soft yet purposeful position. For the purpose of this analysis they are described as 'prairie runs'. The music builds for this section (a bar of accents leading into *ff* in the score), which is danced by three dancers, structured into a duet, followed by a solo, continuing with the duet, returning to the soloist and concluding with the duet again. This structure can be described as a

● Task 4, p. 96.   variation of a rondo form (a, b, a1, b1, a2, c):

(a) Douglas and Quinn enter with the 'prairie runs'. The music softens as Douglas helps Quinn into a deep lunge followed by a series of counterbalances, counterpulls, supports and lifts. The first music returns for more 'prairie runs'. Douglas initiates a more intimate duet as he moves Quinn by the elbow. In closer contact, they wind and unwind through and around each other. Once more the running music returns, and Quinn turns to follow Douglas who leads the 'prairie runs'. There is a sense of care,

● Task 5, p. 96.   support and equality in the duets, but before the dancers have time to take much rest, the music urges them on, propelling them back into travelling, circling around the space to keep moving on. This sub-section concludes with Quinn 'knocking' Douglas's back with a loose fist. This 'knocking' gesture is seen in many of Davies's works, in modified yet related ways, with different intensity and purpose, often performed by a solo dancer knocking into the air or on an imaginary surface, rather than in a duet (for example in *Sphinx*, *Sounding* and *The Art of Touch*).

(b) The lighting change, the change to a more sparse sound, and music marked *pp*, all bring about a very different mood and quality. Attention is

Catherine Quinn in rehearsal.
(Part 2, Section A.)
Photo: David Buckland

The opening of the Second Dance in Volans's score.   © Chester Music Ltd. Reproduced by permission.

Part 2: A Summary

	Section A group	Section B trio (Douglas, Quinn, Clark)
	Subsections: a duet b solo c solo a1 duet	Subsections: a duet b solo a1 duet b1 solo a2 duet c duet
Key Motifs	• animal head • tomahawk • sky and earth • framing face • counterpull attitude	• framing face
Action Content	As Part 1, plus: • more turning • more transferences of weight • twists, spirals, lunges • counterpulls	As Part 1, plus: • 'prairie runs' • knocking gesture • more change in supports and use of supports, and higher lifts • fluid twists, spirals, lunges • 'limb tracing'
Dynamic Content	• bold and purposeful • soft and fluid • following breath rhythm and accents/cues in the music	• merging with, then separating from the music • soft and fluid • swinging, lilting • bold, accented
Spatial Content	• circular floor patterns • travels across the stage • diagonal counterpull • facing diagonals	• circular floor patterns • diagonal line of travel
Thematic Content	• continuing as Part 1 • Clark emerging as an individual	• continuing as Part 1 • Clark's distance/separation from the group • confident travelling over a long distance • playfulness

now on Scott Clark, who dances a fluid solo, folding, twisting, spiralling and lunging, punctuated by the arms lengthening away from the body as if throwing energy outwards, clearly reflecting the rhythm in the music. The circular, continuous motion of Clark as he travels gradually across the diagonal emphasises Clark's individuality in the dance, and at times his separation or distance from the rest of the group.

(a1) The lights intensify for a return to the 'prairie run' music, followed by a softer duet section. Focus is on hands tracing limbs; elbows are soft, hinged, jointed. The 'prairie runs' return, with slight variation, and then a livelier, more dynamic series of new lifts completes this sub-section. The section ends with Quinn 'knocking' on Douglas' back, as before.

(b1) This is a direct repeat of (b) except that Clark dances his solo facing a new front and is filmed with images of Douglas and Quinn projected in front of him, Quinn continuing the 'knocking' on Douglas's back. This reinforces the contrast between the contact between the couple, at rest, and Clark's continuously moving, loose-limbed solo.

▶ Film/Dance Dialogue, p. 62.

(a2) This is a very brief duet for Douglas and Quinn, combining leans and lifts with the tactile 'limb tracing' material seen before in this part.

(c) The final music change (marked *ppp*) brings Fulwell and Potter back for a duet: a slower repeat of material from Section A. Potter slips off stage in silence from under Fulwell's extended arm, leaving Fulwell alone.

Part 3

Section A

▶ Lighting, p. 54.

Fulwell begins with a solo danced to the sparse sound of the *pizzicato* cello solo. Visually we see both dancer and cellist, both moving together, a new partnership. Fulwell moves fluidly into and out of the floor, hanging from extended limbs before falling off-balance into deep lunges, rarely stopping until finally coming to rest sitting, legs outstretched, on the floor.

Section B

▶ Film/Dance Dialogue, p. 61.

● Task 6, p. 96.

The solo cello continues, although the sound is richer, as the other two men join for a trio which moves in simple canon across the stage, once more emphasising the sense of travel across the space. The men dance into and out of the floor, suggesting an easy, comfortable relationship with the ground, jointed and fluid, combining sweeps, curves and gentle turns. This is the only time we see the men dance together as a trio.

Section C

▶ Key Motifs, p. 74.

Before long the women enter, passing through and between the men, for a short ensemble section, ending with the *animal head* motif, leaving Potter standing alone. The other instruments return.

Section D

▶ Film/Dance Dialogue, p. 61.

▶ Key Motifs, p. 77.

Potter concludes this part with a sensuous solo which moves around the edges of the space, restating the sense of travel and the marking out of territory. In it we see much material from earlier in the dance, including a development of the *framing face* motif which begins and concludes the solo. Movement is sinewy, her body folds and reaches, skims and darts

Rehearsal picture of Michael Fulwell's solo opening Part 3. Photo: David Buckland

across the floor with soft limbs and hinged elbows, twisting, spiralling and moving continuously until it resolves to a counterpull or stillness. There are flurries of faster movement; but as much of the movement at this point is slower, more sustained, linear and extended, there is more time to see shifts of weight and use of counterpull in the body.

● Notation Task 1, p. 99.
Notation Task 3, p. 99.

The opening of the Third Dance in Volans's score.   © Chester Music Ltd. Reproduced by permission.

Part 3: A Summary

	Section A solo (Fulwell)	**Section B** men's trio	**Section C** group	**Section D** solo (Potter)
Key Motifs		• animal head	• counterpull attitude	• tailbone–back • framing face • counterpull attitude
Action Content	• neutral body alignment and relaxed body attitude • balance to off-balance • extension	• moving into and out of the floor • curves, turns • balance to off-balance	as Part 1, plus: • moving into and out of the floor • curves, turns • balance to off-balance	as Part 1, plus: • more closing and opening • focus more on torso and different surfaces or parts of the body • use of counterpull
Dynamic Content	• fluid • continuous	• fluid • continuous • swings	• fluid • continuous • swings • rebounds	• as before with more use of weight and increased dynamic range • echoing the sustained and pizzicato musical themes
Spatial Content	• high to low	• travelling across the stage, side to side	• travelling across the stage, side to side, and covering the whole stage space	• travelling around the edges of the space
Thematic Content	• partnership between dancer and cellist	• men – moving with stealth	• the group re-established	• covering space, sense of a journey

Part 4

Section A

This part begins with a contemplative, private solo, danced by Scott Clark. The music is more sustained, with *legato* strings, and subdued lighting suggests warmth. The camera follows arms, hands and face rather than the whole body, which emphasises the tactile, intimate nature and quality of the solo. Clark follows the theme developed by Potter as he traces the length of his own arms; his hands touch and frame his own face, his elbows are soft, emphasising joints, arms making circular sweeps. His own focus alternates from watching his own body moving, to directed more outwards into space. He moves into and out of the floor; he lies and rests, but travels little through space.

● Task 7, p. 96.

▶ A Dance in Time, p. 5. Film/Dance Dialogue, p. 64.

Section B

Potter joins Clark, and as a duet they continue with tactile, sensuous material, emphasising touch, skin contact, pouring weight and tracing the length of limbs as if to explore the distance between two extremities – head and foot, arm and leg. The duet includes soft, effortless, gentle lifts, nudging and folding over each other, which suggests the duet may have developed out of improvisation, based on the principles of contact improvisation. Elements of their own solo material from earlier in the dance are seen again, now placed together in space.

● Task 8, p. 96.

Section C

Fulwell enters and Potter joins him, leaving Clark briefly separated, alone again. The duet melts into a lilting trio with Clark, travelling across the stage in unison, introducing fragments of a new travelling phrase, leading into a simple walk, while the arms gesture in continuous, circular motions. The other dancers join and the unison travelling phrase begins again, moving more energetically across the stage, yet still with the same

The opening of the Fourth Dance in Volans's score.   © Chester Music Ltd. Reproduced by permission.

Part 4: A Summary

	Section A solo (Clark)	Section B duet (Potter, Clark)	Section C group
Key Motifs	• animal head • framing face now linked	• framing face	• animal head • tailbone–back • tomahawk • shoulder shake • framing face
Action Content	• continuous touch • sequential • centrally initiated • attention taken away from steps due to rhythm • resting	• 'limb tracing' • nudging, 'grazing', pouring weight in partnering	as Part 1, plus: • sequential • gestural • centrally initiated • travelling
Dynamic Content	• lots of continuous rhythm, no accent or punctuation • swing and impulse doesn't give into gravity	• continuous • no accent or punctuation	• fluid, rippling, seamless, lilting
Spatial Content	• circles • moving into the floor and out again	• moving around, between and through	• moving across, side to side • circles in the body
Thematic Content	• Clark as an individual • private, tactile, attention on skin, muscle, contours of the body, heat	• Clark in partnership – supportive but vulnerable • equality in lifting and weight sharing • care, co-operation	• the community re-established • individual statements • continuous travelling/journeying

seamless, sweeping, rippling quality, moving from side to side, emphasising the continuous journey, rarely coming to rest. As the group travel continues, each dancer emerges in turn for a brief solo. This is an opportunity to see clearly the personal movement phrases which have been transformed and rearranged throughout the dance, emphasising each dancer's individual presence in the dance. The part concludes as it began, with solo material danced by Clark, but this time with material seen before in his solos in Part 2, in the 'knocking' sections.

▶ A Dance in Time, p. 6.
Film/Dance Dialogue,
pp. 63–4.

▶ Music/Dance
Dialogue, p. 46.
Interpreting the Work,
p. 109.

▶ Following the Work,
p. 83.

Scott Clark and Lauren Potter.
(Part 4, Section B.)
Photo: David Buckland

The opening of the Fifth Dance in Volans's score.   © Chester Music Ltd. Reproduced by permission.

Part 5: A Summary

group (a, b, c, d)

Subsections:
  a   group
  b   quartet
  c   quartet
  d   group

Key
Motifs
  • animal head
  • tailbone–back
  • tomahawk
  • shoulder shake
  • sky and earth
  • counterpull attitude

Action
Content
  • gestures
  • low elevation, skimming the floor
  • faster travelling
  • centrally initiated/torso initiated pathways within the body
  • quick succession of body parts/highly articulate
  • neutral body alignment and relaxed body attitude
  • partnering (lifts, balances)
  • stillness
  • more sense of arrival

Dynamic
Content
  • mirroring the music (pulse, speed, accent) and contrasting the music (e.g. stillness without silence)
  • sense of urgency/anticipation
  • playfulness

Spatial
Content
  • circles
  • travelling across the stage – side to side
  • covering the whole stage space
  • exiting 'downstage' (towards the camera)

Thematic
Content
  • playful, gamelike, yet with tension, urgency and expectancy
  • sense of community
  • calm, fragmented close – as if motion continuing

Part 5

The change in music brings about the clearest change in mood and atmosphere in this, the final part of the dance. Played by the viola and cello, the music has a deeper, jagged, vibratory sound. The part begins with film of the musicians, which is then projected behind the dancers for the first few bars. Douglas and Quinn enter, falling forward into a low *arabesque*, one leg stretched behind as the opposite arm circles overhead towards the floor. The rest of the group join for duets, trios and quartets. The music builds, tension increases, and movement phrases appear shorter, marked more by stillness. Motifs seen earlier in the dance combine with new, previously unseen, livelier material. Despite this new sense of urgency, there is a playful, game-like quality as each dancer takes over from another dancer to continue a duet, or moves to initiate a duet with a dancer who is at rest. Camera angles give new perspectives on the action as dancers run towards and past the camera to leave the stage area, reinforcing the multi-layered structure of the work. The *animal head* motif is seen clearly, as in Part 1, but here it is more accented, mirroring the pulse in the music. The film focuses on the musicians' fingers on the strings while the dancers pause; then the dancers move again, as if dancing on the bridge of the viola.

▶ Film/Dance Dialogue, p. 61.

▶ Film/Dance Dialogue, pp. 61–2.

▶ Key Motifs, p. 74.

● Task 9, 96.

One by one the dancers gradually come to rest in the space, either alone or with a partner, leaving Douglas to conclude the dance with the same movement that opens this part, a low suspended *arabesque* hovering in space, the arm again circling overhead. The final film image is of the musicians, also coming to rest. This quiet resolution to the dance avoids a climactic finish and is a familiar Davies device. She generally avoids any predictable, conclusive ending, such as massing groups together for a large unison section, or making sculptural groupings. She frequently dims the light on moving bodies, communicating the idea of the human body in continual motion.

▶ Interpreting the Work, p. 105.

● Task 10, pp. 96–7.

Tasks

1. Dancers are 'complex instruments' with different personalities and idiosyncrasies. Consider ways in which this can be both a challenge and a gift for a choreographer.

2. Study the visual images and the associated descriptions for the key motifs in *White Man Sleeps*. (a) Select three or more and find different ways of moving into and out of the motifs. (b) Using only the descriptive names of three or more of the motifs, devise your own movement motifs. (c) Link together the material you have made into a seamless whole.

3. Devise a short movement p'ırase which can be performed by three or more dancers. Explore the many ways in which the material can be structured into canon form. Explore ways in which the canon material can be structured to communicate the sense of travel. Try setting the material on circular pathways and linear pathways. What are the different effects produced?

4. Devise a short movement study using the same rondo form.

5. Working with a partner, each make a short solo movement phrase. Mark out a small area of the studio, and find ways of dancing your own phrases within this space, retaining where possible the same rhythmic structure of your own material. Find moments of contact, weight-taking, counterpoint and synchronicity. Now enlarge the area and find different ways of setting the duet together.

6. Devise a movement phrase which includes the following: up to down, sweeping, curving, gentle turning, side to side.

7. Sketch and identify the bones and joints in the arms, up to and including the shoulder girdle. Describe ways in which Davies's use of the arms in *White Man Sleeps* can be said to be different to the way the arms are used in classical ballet, Graham technique or Cunningham technique.

8. Working with a partner, improvise dancing together using the ideas of nudging, pouring, folding, opening and closing, and exchanging weight, using both contact and weight-bearing.

9. Listen carefully to the music in this part. What images, moods or ideas does the music suggest to you? Devise a short study exploring these suggestions.

10. There are many ways in which charts and other diagrammatic representations of a dance can help to trace the development and structure of a dance. Many aspects of *White Man Sleeps* can be selected and focused on in this way, which, either individually or collectively, can help to build up a picture of the dance as a whole. The chart

Scott Clark's Role Through the Dance

Part	Section	Sub-section	Clark's Role
1	A		Dances with opening trio
	B		
	C		Dances with the group
2	A	a	
		b	Dances solo material for first time (with others dancing), marked by dramatic change in light and sound
	B	a1	
		a	
		b	Solo – a dramatic change in light and music, quieter, shadowy
		a1	
		b1	Solo repeated to a new front – sense of distance/separation emphasised
		a2	
		c	
3	A		
	B		Dances with men in trio – an equal role
	C		Dances with the group, but slightly separated at times
	D		
4	A		Lights warm, subdued, extended solo, repeated material, moving in own space
	B		Duet with Potter – same dynamic as in solo
	C		Briefly separated but becomes part of group. The part ends with Clark's solo material from Part 2B, subsection (b)
5		a	
		b	
		c	Absent from the quartet
		d	Returns, quietly, reintegrated

above, tracing Scott Clark's role through the dance, is one such example, and is adapted from a similar chart devised by Pauline Hodgens. Clark, who seems to have a special role within the dance, is the focus for this analysis.

There are many possible aspects of the dance that could be charted in this way, for example: (a) floor patterns/spatial design; (b) use of unison or canon; (c) who dances a particular motif and gesture, at what times; (d) the duet form. Choose one of these topics, or select a theme of your own, and make a chart similar to the one shown for Scott Clark's role. What does this tell you about the dance? How it is made? What are the effects?

→ Hodgens, 'The Choreographic Structure of Robert Cohan's *Stabat Mater* (1975)'.

Notation Tasks

A Note on Labanotation

Systems of dance notation have existed for many centuries, usually developed in response to a specific dance style. Labanotation is a system of symbols used to describe movement of the body conceived by Rudolf Laban and first published in 1928. Laban developed his notation using a spatial and anatomical model of human movement and therefore the system is able to record the full range of movement possibilities.

The system relies on a basic unit or symbol placed on a vertical staff. Each symbol provides four bits of information. Its placement on the staff shows which part of the body is moving. The shape of the symbol and its shading shows the direction and level that the body part moves in, and the length of the symbol shows the length of time the action takes to complete.

Laban developed several approaches for looking at movement. Labanotation provides a structural description, an accurate depiction of the body moving through space and within a specific time frame. 'Effort' analysis provides a qualitative description of movement and focuses on the use of energy throughout a given action. Effort analysis categorises dynamic qualities into space, time, weight and flow and records these with symbols for the two extremes within each category.

The Labanotation included within this book is written at elementary standard. This level is universally recognised, and the A-level dance syllabus covers the same material. Therefore, certain descriptive choices have been made when notating the vocabulary. While keeping as true to the performance as possible, the notation has been simplified to a form that A-level students and elementary notators can understand and utilise. Choices have also been made concerning which dancer to notate, as there are variations in the material between the dancers due to individuality and personal style.

The notated *motifs* (pp. 74–7) show snapshots of a position reached within a continuously moving phrase. The accompanying photographs illustrate the motifs too, but are not necessarily identical to the Labanotation.

The notated *phrases* enable the reader to embody the movement style in *White Man Sleeps*. The sections notated have been selected to show repeated motifs and movement style without incorporating material that is beyond the elementary syllabus. Effort analysis has been included alongside each extract, recording predominant dynamics for particular actions. The sections notated are: (1) the *sky and earth* travelling phrase, initially performed in a straight line. This section is also seen throughout the dance, often performed in a circular pathway (p. 76); (2) the phrase that begins with the *tomahawk* motif, into the *shoulder shake* and finishes with the *animal head*, seen throughout the dance, but introduced in Part 1 (p. 100); (3) the basic phrase that begins Lauren Potter's solo at the end of Part 3 of the dance, beginning and ending with the *framing face* motif (p. 101).

Tasks

Refer to the Labanotation Glossary on p. 102 for help.

1. There are three notated excerpts: the *sky and earth* travelling phrase (p. 76); the phrase that begins with the *tomahawk* motif, into the *shoulder shake*, and finishes with the *animal head* motif, introduced in Part 1, and seen throughout the dance (p. 100); and the basic phrase that begins Lauren Potter's solo at the end of Part 3 of the dance, beginning and ending with the *framing face* motif (p. 101).

For each excerpt: (a) Reconstruct the support column. (b) Find the sections in the video and listen to the rhythm of the music. With the music, or with a metronome set to the appropriate speed, rehearse the rhythm of the supports moving through space. (c) Reconstruct each phrase with both supports and gestures. (d) Observe each phrase or motif throughout the whole dance and note their repetitions and variations. (e) Look at each individual performing the same phrase. How do they differ? Are the steps or the dynamics different? (f) Video your class performing each phrase. Observe your own personal dynamics.

2. Create a travel phrase yourself in the same 13-count measure as the *sky and earth* phrase (p. 76). Juxtapose your phrase with the original to create a short dance of your own in 13/4.

3. The overall impression of Lauren Potter's solo is of quiet, calm travel, but on closer inspection there are a lot of very quick small steps and jumps. After reconstructing the notated phrase (opposite), create a phrase of your own that evokes a sense of calm, by quickly skimming across the floor.

Notated phrase including the *tomahawk*, *shoulder shake* and *animal head* motifs, first introduced in Part 1 of the dance.

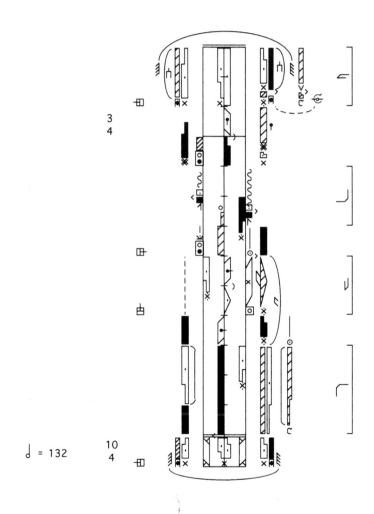

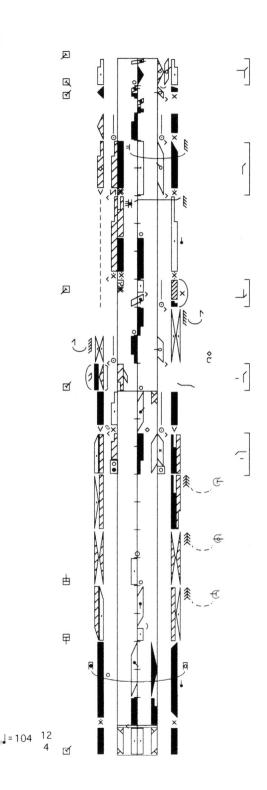

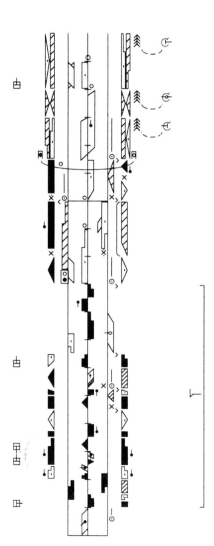

Notated phrase that begins Lauren
Potter's solo at the end of Part 3.

♩= 104 12/4

Labanotation Glossary

    The upper body is included in the gesture for the arm.

    Curve the torso over the front surface.

    Shaking, as seen in shaking the shoulders in the excerpt on p. 100.

    Palm of the hand is near the top of the head.

    The action of the arm is led by the fingertips, as seen in the *animal head* motif.

    Hands are near the left ear, as seen in the Lauren Potter's solo excerpt (p. 101).

   Palm of the left hand touches back of right hand.

    Right hand is supporting the leg from the underside of the lower leg, as seen in Lauren Potter's solo excerpt (p. 101).

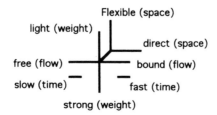   'Effort' graph.

Part 5
Open Endings

Sanjoy Roy

Interpreting White Man Sleeps

Scott Clark's solo, Part 4.
Photo: David Buckland.

Interpreting the Work

White Man Sleeps is 'open-ended' in two senses. On one level, as with many of Davies's works, it defers a sense of final resolution: the dance 'fades out', drawing quietly to a close and continuing to reverberate in the imagination after the movement has finished. On another level, the meanings of the dance are also open-ended, working on the imagination through allusion and connotation rather than by definition and resolution.

▶ Following the Work, p. 95.

What, then, is White Man Sleeps about? The question is much less easy to answer with an 'abstract' dance such as White Man Sleeps than with a narrative or dramatic dance. The preceding chapters, while providing many points of interpretation, have focused more on how the dance is made than on what it means. In doing so, we hope to have illustrated the following points on how its possible meanings are generated:

→ Roy, 'Expanding the Human Body'.

■ The dance operates simultaneously on a number of different levels. On the level of *content*, the elements of movement, music, design and so on are assembled together in fluid, shifting interactions. The dance also operates on the level of *context*, which includes that of the individual viewer, its place in the development of Davies's choreographic career, within contemporary dance practice in Britain, and within the wider context of arts, culture and society. There are, as Davies says, 'several layers of entry into the piece'. Any of these different levels can provide such an entry, a perspective on the dance, and all can be said to *influence* our interpretations without *determining* them.

▶ Collaborations, pp. 33–64. Contents, pp. 69–95.

▶ Contexts, pp. 13–28.

▶ A Dance in Time, p. 7.

■ Just as it operates on a number of different levels, the dance also *communicates* simultaneously on different levels. We often tend to think of meanings by analogy with language, with words and vocabulary. While this is a fruitful metaphor, it is also important to remember that dance is a non-verbal medium, and it communicates through different senses: visually, through its imagery, designs and lighting; aurally, through its sounds and score; and kinaesthetically, through the corporeal feel of the movement quality, shape, effort and weight. In fact, language communicates not simply verbally (as text) but also non-verbally (as utterance), through its rhythm, intonation, pitch, timbre and volume; and particularly with a non-narrative dance such as *White Man Sleeps*, this often parallels the way that movement communicates more closely, through its phrasing, dynamics, pacing and energy.

● Task 1, p. 111.

■ The meanings of the dance are generated by analogy with the way that is made: through a process of collaboration and dialogue. Just as the collaborators and the different media have their own contributions to the dance, so do its meanings emerge in relation with the audience, who find their own 'layers of entry' into the piece. As with the creative process, Davies is concerned with the connections that emerge, more interested in dialogues than in statements.

▶ Dialogues in Dance, pp. 33–4.

▶ Lyric Television, p. 64.

● Task 2, p. 111.

Though the meanings of the dance are 'open', they are not arbitrary. A valid interpretation will have a basis in the work itself, and by exploring what is going on in the dance, on the levels of content or context, more can be discovered to enrich and support our interpretations. Below is one example of an interpretation of how the dancers are 'characterised' as human beings. It is presented here as one possible 'take' on the dance – but it is one possibility among many, neither definitive nor exhaustive.

An Example: 'Characterising' White Man Sleeps

As with many 'abstract' dances, *White Man Sleeps* nevertheless evokes a sense of a particular social world. Though the dancers are not given specific characters or scenarios, the dance does convey several levels of characterisation and interaction:

■ *Internal*. One task set to the dancers in *White Man Sleeps* was to explore complex pathways of motion within the body: imagining an impulse of movement travelling inside the body, flowing through the spine, wrapping round the ribs, or eddying through joints. This can be seen clearly in the opening section, in phrases which include the *animal head*, *tomahawk*, *shoulder shake* and *tailbone–back* motifs. The dynamic is fluid and continuous, the movement is unprojected. The movement seems visceral and interior, arising from deep within the body; it is not projected outwards or 'displayed' to the audience. The effect is sensual, internal, private, suggesting an inner complexity but one that is calm and at ease, not conflictual or anxious.

▶ Key Motifs, pp. 74–5. Following the Work, p. 79.

■ *Personal*. The idea of personal characterisation is perhaps most clearly seen in solos, such as Lauren Potter's long solo which ends Part 3, with its free, expansive motion around the stage combined with soft, luxuriant curves and extensions of the spine; or Scott Clark's subsequent solo in Part 4, not travelling at all, but enclosed, moving between upright and lying. The impression of individuality is also communicated through associating the different dancers with particular phrases of movement. Catherine Quinn's phrase that first appears in Part 2, combines *framing face* gestures with leans and lunges, and has a halting, hesitant quality, brought up short at the end of phrases. The different movement phrases associated with different dancers 'characterise' them as individuals with personal qualities, without giving them specific characters as such.

▶ Following the Work, pp. 88–9.

▶ Following the Work, p. 91.

▶ Key Motifs, p. 77. Following the Work, p. 83.

■ *Interpersonal*. Other points in the dance emphasise interpersonal relations. This is perhaps most easily seen in duets. The duet for Catherine Quinn and Paul Douglas in Part 2 moves between bounding, playful runs, through to more intimate gestures of care and touch – echoing the shifts in music from weightily bowed strings to a quieter legato melody. The different qualities of movement and partnering in this duet suggest different layers to the relationship; but on each level it is consensual, empathetic. Contrast this, for example, with the duet for Lauren Potter and Michael Fulwell that opens Part 2. Potter and Fulwell have already been paired in

▶ Following the Work, p. 83.

Paul Old and Gill Clarke,
in the 1997 version.
Photo: Sean Hudson

▶ Following the Work,
p. 91.

Part 1 in a supportive, co-operative duet, but in Part 2, the partnering is less harmonious: Potter reaches out in one direction, to be pulled back; during a lift, she stiffens her body out straight, halting the flow of movement. Both these duets contrast with that for Potter and Scott Clark in Part 4, which is much slower, more contained – without moving much in space – and also more tender (again echoing the quality of music).

■ *Social.* While maintaining a sense of individuality, the dancers nevertheless appear to belong to the same community. Their costumes are unified in style, though not uniform. There is frequent use of canon, in which the same movement material is shared amongst dancers, but overlapped and separated on the stage, which again underscores the separateness of the dancers while identifying them as belonging together. Perhaps the clearest demonstration, though, occurs in the 'travelling' sequence that finishes Part 4. Here, the dancers move as a group from which a series of solos emerges, each showing some of the individual, personal phrases that have been seen earlier, before merging back into the ensemble. In this way, the dancers retain separate individual identities within an overall sense of belonging to a group.

▶ Following the Work, pp. 91–3.

In *White Man Sleeps*, Davies holds in balance several different layers of 'characterisation', which range from the internal, through the individual, to the interpersonal and social. By interweaving material from all of these levels into different contexts, the dance generates a sense of community to which all the dancers clearly belong, while also suggesting varied interactions, maintaining individuality, and evoking private worlds and personal memories. The overall impression is that these characterisations are gentle, considerate and empathetic: not only human, but also humane. These meanings are evoked not through statements and explicit references, but rather through the form of the dance itself – its divisions into solos, duets and groups, the sharing and variation of movement material, the dynamics of action and partnering.

● Task 3, p. 111.

→ Roy, 'Human and Exacting'.

It is noticeable that the 1997 version of the dance created a slightly different impression. Since the original version, Davies has developed the idea of complex internal pathways of motion. Where in the original *White Man Sleeps* they are fluid and sinuous, in *Wild Translations* (1995) she deliberately made those paths run counter to their natural sense of phrasing, interrupting them, reversing them, or veering them off in unexpected directions. This gave a sharper and sometimes more awkward edge to the movement, as well as providing a more demanding challenge to the dancers' dexterity. Compositionally, too, Davies has developed the complexity of groupings and canons, with a more intricate attention to their spacing and timing. These qualities can be seen in many of her recent works, and also in the 1997 reworking of *White Man Sleeps*, in which the phrasing is

▶ Physical Puzzles, pp. 17–18.

● Task 4, p. 111.

▶ A Dance in Time, p. 8. Reworkings, p. 19. White Man Sleeps Revisited, pp. 47–8.

more punctuated and varied, the partnerwork more complex, and the groupings more detailed. The 'community' of dancers in this version seems more separated, their interactions more taut.

The theme of 'characterisation' has been chosen here because Davies frequently seems concerned with balancing ideas of belonging and togetherness with individual differences and private, inner worlds. It also illustrates how the form of the dance can be richly suggestive of ideas and feelings without specifically referring to them. Nevertheless, it is only one aspect of the dance: there are many other 'entry points' for interpretation, and the idea of a 'social world' in the dance provides only one possible framework.

White Man Sleeps, as with Davies's work in general, suggests far more than it states: the performers seem to be dancing on the very cusp of possibility. As much as their physical presence, and that of the designs and music, it is the depth of that possibility, its tug on the imagination, that draws the viewer in.

The form of this book, too, is open. The different chapters offer a variety of angles on the piece, while the marginal cross-references indicate some of its various entry (or exit) points, and provide alternative routes to follow through the web of interconnections which make up the work. Readers, teachers and students alike are encouraged to pursue their own interests, moving between text, table, task, image and notation as they choose. Thus, in addition to providing a thorough factual account of the making of *White Man Sleeps*, we hope that the book may also act as a stimulus for creative, imaginative exploration.

Tasks

1. Is there such a thing as a 'language of movement'? How far is language a useful model for non-verbal communication through movement? What other models of communication are there? Are different models of communication appropriate for different styles of dance?

2. Look at the press reviews in the appendices (pp. 115–19). What aspects of the dance to the reviewers pick out? Are there differences between them? Compare the reviews for the 1988 and 1997 versions.

3. Look at *Wyoming* by Siobhan Davies, and another piece of 'abstract' dance by a different choreographer. What levels of 'social world' do they convey? Compare them with *White Man Sleeps*, illustrating your opinions with examples from the pieces. You might consider the following: the uniformity or diversity of movement; the role that individual dancers play; the organisation of groups; the differentiation of gender; the style of partnering; the style of presentation to the audience.

4. Imagine a pathway of travelling within your body. Allow an impulse of movement to flow along it, trying to make the movement as precise but as seamless as possible, so that it seems fluid and natural. Now identify particular moments where you could interrupt the flow, or change its direction or dynamic. What are the different feelings communicated by the types of movement?

Appendices

Press Reviews
Biographies
Production Credits
Choreography by Siobhan Davies
Siobhan Davies Dance Company
Key Sources and Bibliography

Scott Clark and Lauren Potter.
(Part 4.)
Photo: David Buckland

Press Reviews

1988

Kathrine Sorley Walker
Daily Telegraph, 11 November 1988
Back from America after a study break on a Fulbright Arts Fellowship, Siobhan Davies, one of our most gifted modern dance choreographers, launched her new group at Riverside Studios, Hammersmith, on Wednesday. The programme, specially commissioned by Dance Umbrella, immediately set a high standard of composition and performance. Reliance on dance, with admirably chosen music and design and without recourse to provocative gimmicks or obscure emotional content, produced two new and satisfying works.

Davies's career goes back to the origins of London Contemporary Dance Theatre in 1969 and she began creating dance works as early as 1971. Always stylish and fluent, Davies seems now to have an added facility for variety of pace and dramatic colouring.

The first piece, *Wyoming*, to music by Jean Marc Gowans, opened with a soft mist drifting across the stage while each of the dancers performed introductory solos. A sense of lethargy suggested open spaces and hot temperatures.

The three men – Michael Fulwell, Scott Clark and Paul Douglas – had athletic, free-flowing movements ranging over the whole performing area. Lauren Potter was given a lighter, speedier and more circling dance and Gill Clarke, in a splendid sequence, was concerned with maintained poses linked by jumps and single handed springs. At last the separate strands were brought together.

This was a good work but it was surpassed by the other production. *White Man Sleeps* took its title from Kevin Volans' engaging string quartet on which it was based, and which was played by the Degas String Quartet.

The score was brilliantly reflected by Davies in sections of duet, trio and solo, delicately shaded in mood and tempi. A strong and sprightly duet with forceful leaps and lifts was complemented by a tender pas de deux featuring smooth partnering and gentle explorations of faces and limbs. This extended into a more allegro trio and later into a brisk and joyous quartet.

Davies's sustained dance inventiveness and perceptive use of music – qualities all too rarely found in choreographers – established her as a leader in her field. The dancers are already a proficient team and all the artistic ingredients now exists for a notable group future.

John Percival
The Times, 11 November 1988
You have only three more nights, ending on Sunday, November 13, to see two of the best dance works made in Britain all year; otherwise you must wait until next spring to see them on Channel 4 or next summer for a tour. The choreographer, Siobhan Davies, who is now back in action after a sabbatical year, is most certainly on a winning streak.

The new company she has assembled consists of just six first rate dancers. Both the new works she has made for them are in the form that generally suits her best; pieces with no visible story line but a great deal of individual character in the dances.

In *Wyoming* the thought that came to mind as I watched the dancers hungrily exploring space was (as with Davies's *Embarque*, which was created for Rambert Dance Company) of the opening up of America.

Not that there is much in the movement that is specific to that theme: arms swinging as if to whip on a horse, perhaps, in a lively trio for Lauren Potter with Michael Fulwell and Paul Douglas, and a sense of wearily settling down after a long journey in the final duet for Gill Clarke and Scott Clark.

But David Buckland's setting, mainly a floorcloth painted like a simple map reinforces this idea; so does the steady drive of John Marc Gowans's soundtrack, relieved at one point by voices, rounded off by a rush of water.

The other work, *White Man Sleeps*, takes it title and shape from the music, a thrilling modern string quartet by Kevin Volans. Riverside cannot run to the Kronos quartet, who introduced it to London audiences, but it is played with great spirit by the Degas quartet.

The idiosyncratic motifs of arms held forward or hands circling round a face sometimes seemed to promise a specific meaning that is not delivered. Otherwise the movement develops mainly as a reaction to a strong, fascinating score. Its shape, like that of the five solos which begin *Wyoming*, is in an idiom familiar in Davies's work, instinctive movement growing from moments of stillness, but the contrasts of speed, texture, direction and patterning are worked through with new mastery. See it.

Stephanie Jordan
Dance Theatre Journal (1989) Vol. 6 No. 4.

Almost two years ago, Siobhan Davies made her last work for LCDT, *Red Steps*, a thoroughly confident and admirable construction, performed in that inimitable luscious-but-laboured LCDT style, but not a piece to reach your heart. Since she returned from her Fulbright Fellowship on the US, a time for 'living' as well as studying, our eyes have been trained anxiously, looking for the refreshed Davies, a startling new chapter in the choreographer's book, believing, for good reason, that if what was hoped for did happen, the results could be exceptionally exciting. Already, reports of her new *Embarque* for Rambert (which I have not yet seen) have been glowing, rapturous even, but the crucial step forward must be the formation of the choreographer's own enterprise, the Siobhan Davies Company, five dancers, and, with the exception of Lauren Potter, none of them of the familiar 'Davies team'. Dance Umbrella commissioned Davies to present a new programme of work for the festival, and she came up with *Wyoming* and *White Man Sleeps*. [. . .]

Davies also found useful her experience in the US doing classes that weren't concerned with styled technique like ballet, Cunningham and Graham, but with making your own movement choices from images and sensations (work allied to contact and release traditions). This too has informed the dancers, with the exception of Scott Clark, all schooled traditionally and new to this approach.

Davies has given Clark a major role in this programme, a gesture in no way blatant, but you do find him partnering the main duets of both pieces, and in *White Man Sleeps* he has a series of curious up-the-back solos, rather in the spirit of the wild ace that he really is. It is good to see Clark now in work other than his own (or Suzie Ater's). Davies has given him material with an edge that was often wanting in his own, and yet there's an interesting tension between him and the group, perhaps because the danger of him keeling over into too personal a style seems so imminent. With Davies he is contained enough to belong to a community, but only just, and at present, she teems to be using to advantage the precariousness of that situation.

Alas, the fifth member of Davies' group, Lizie Saunderson, broke her foot one week before opening night, and the two dancers who leapt in to fill her part in each work (Gill Clarke in *Wyoming* and Catherine Quinn in *White Man Sleeps*) have to be praised for absorbing so intelligently and thoroughly what was made, with an unusual degree of intimacy, on someone else. But it is clear that all the dancers have been enriched by their experience of this new work, and you could see, even more so by the third performance, a depth of identification with their movement that is rare, and moving.

In *White Man Sleeps*, the movement is sprung from the same basis of physical sensation [as *Wyoming*], 'internalized movement', yet this is definitely the extrovert piece of the two. You don't sense the same intensity of physical experience deeply considered within the moment of performance itself. There isn't time for this: the drive of the movement rhythms and of the music provide the pressure here (gentle but insistent African-influenced impulses – Kevin Volans's first String Quartet *White Man Sleeps* played live by the Degas Quartet) and there is less focus on the qualities of the single body. Instead more abstract dance values emerge, the fluctuations of textural density, between small and large movement, unison and counterpoint, crowd and duet/solo combinations, compact and fragmented stage pictures, even movement in circles, or straight, sharp lines. That is how you can interpret the fundamental travelling phrase of the first section; it ripples merrily, the pelvis circles, then there is some kind of light jiggle of the shoulders – and a lot more that I can't recall – and the momentum suddenly calms into an arrow-sharp double-arm gesture forwards, palms pressing up/down against each other. It is as if design has absorbed all impetus for motion.

Yet the heart of the work (and the most interesting feature of it) is again very sensual and very private, centering on Potter and Scott Clark, in solos, then in partnership, dancers who become people. Their gestures close in and become more specific; they brush a hand along the inside of the opposite arm, press lightly against a cheek or forehead, or pat the spot just above the ankle, and together that touching seems to enclose the other person as if they become one. Soon afterwards, when that private detail is transmitted to the rest of the group, it adopts a more decorative tone. The end (the fifth movement of Volans's quartet) flies out again, larger movement, larger space, recollections of the opening, and eventually the group scattered, caught motionless, save one dancer who is still dancing.

I imagine that the preponderance of small, intimate movement in both these new works will make them ideal television pieces. Immediately after her one week season at Riverside, Davies set to work with lighting designer/TV director Peter Mumford on rethinking this programme for the media. However, as live theatre, this was already the outstanding event of the Umbrella, a familiar spirit renewed – something marvellous to witness – I went back to convince myself that I'd really seen what I thought I'd seen in *Wyoming*. Certainly Davies's evening was one of those occasions when you could leave feeling confident that the Umbrella festival had realized its ambitions.

1997

Judith Mackrell
Guardian, 17 May 1997
It's not often that Davies gives her audience second viewing of her work, but for her current programme she's revived her 1988 piece *White Man Sleeps*, replacing the string quartet version of Kevin Volans's titular score with the original scoring for double harpsichord, viola da gamba and percussion.

The movement in this rich, sensuous dance is tightly wrought, so that gestures brush close to the dancers' bodies or insinuate themselves into the air. A leg or arm may flare out in a bold arc, but they rapidly spring back into place. And with the new scoring, a work that seemed nearly perfect when it was first danced modulates into a wonderful new pitch. The taut resonance of the harpsichord, threaded through with the dark sound of the viola da gamba, concentrates the dance's energy so that it becomes even more densely humming. The stage becomes even more vividly a place of close encounters, glowing surfaces and vibrating shapes, where Davies's marvellous dancers engage with an intimacy that is sometimes dignified, sometimes tender and always gently erotic.

Louise Levene,
Independent, 17 May 1997
On her latest tour, Siobhan Davies has chosen to couple a new work with a revival of her 1988 success *White Man Sleeps*. The original piece was crafted to Kevin Volans's score inspired by his memories of Africa. In 1988, Davies was using the string quartet arrangement of the music but, nine years later, she has chosen Volans's original version for harpsichord, viola da gamba and percussion, a baroque line-up that highlights even more strongly the tension between Volans's Western musical consciousness and the music of his childhood home.

The dancers play in the dappled shade of Peter Mumford's clever lighting design. Occasionally one of the group will spin off into a solo as when Deborah Saxon's arms flurry around her head then snake down her body as if she were alternately donning and shedding the movement like a garment.

Debra Craine
The Times, 20 May 1997
Despite the creative wealth of her back catalogue, Davies is not one for revisiting old territory. There has to be a good reason to revive a work and in the case of *White Man Sleeps*, the other half of her Brighton Festival double bill, the spur was the score.

When Davies choreographed *White Man Sleeps* in 1988, she used Kevin Volans's string quartet of the same name. Nine years later, she has turned to the composer's earlier arrangement of *White Man Sleeps*, scored for two harpsichords, viola da gamba and percussion. It is more abrasive and pungent than the string arrangement, and it gives Davies's choreography even more heft and heart.

She has reworked segments of her original, although the bulk of it remains unchanged. Unlike the more unsettling *Bank*, *White Man Sleeps* seduces its audience with an impulsive sensuality. There is a hedonistic delight in the physicality of Davies's strong-minded dancers, as if they are plunging into a pool of warm, sweetly scented water. It looks a pleasure to dance; it's certainly a pleasure to watch.

Biographies

Siobhan Davies (Choreographer)

Siobhan Davies was one of the first students at London Contemporary Dance School and went on to become a leading dancer and choreographer for London Contemporary Dance Theatre. In 1982, with Richard Alston and Ian Spink, she founded Second Stride, and from 1988 to 1993 she was Associate Choreographer for Rambert Dance Company. She founded Siobhan Davies Dance Company in 1988, on her return from a year in America on a Fulbright Arts Fellowship. 1997 marked the twenty-fifth anniversary of her first professional piece of choreography (*Relay*, for LCDT), and saw her win the Time Out Award for *Bank*. She has received numerous awards, including four Digital Dance Awards, and six nominations for the Prudential Award for Dance, which she won in 1996. She won the Olivier Award for Outstanding Achievement in Dance for *Winnsboro Cotton Mill Blues* and *The Art of Touch* in 1993 and 1996 respectively. *The Art of Touch* also won the 1996 Evening Standard Award for Outstanding Production.

From 1995 to 1997 Davies was Choreographer in Residence and Senior Research Fellow at the Roehampton Institute, London, and in October 1996 she was awarded an Honorary Fellowship from Trinity College of Music, London, in recognition of her creative work with music, both in commissioning new scores for dance and involving live musicians in performance. In June 1995 she was awarded an MBE and in 1999 she was made an Honorary Doctor of the University of Surrey.

Kevin Volans (Composer)

Kevin Volans was born in 1949 in South Africa. From 1973 to 1982 he lived in Cologne, where he was a pupil of the Karlheinz Stockhausen Musikhochschule and later Stockhausen's teaching assistant (1975–76). He also studied with Mauricio Kagel (music theatre), Aloys Kontarsky (piano), and electronic music (1976–80). During this time he worked as a freelance composer, and his work was associated with the so-called New Simplicity. His other activities included four field trips recording African music for German radio. After teaching composition at the University of Natal, he returned to freelance composition, moving to Paris in 1985 and to Ireland in 1986.

Many hundreds of concerts and broadcasts of his work have been given worldwide. Performances in the last few years include the Berliner Festwoche, the Salzburg Festival, Lincoln Center (New York), Next Wave Festival (New York), New Music America (Miami), Interlink Festival (Tokyo), World Music Days (Bonn), Belfast Festival, Adelaide Festival, Montreal Jazz Festival, the Queen Elizabeth Hall and ICA in London, the Turin Opera House, and the Vienna State Opera. Fourteen compact discs featuring his music have been released, one of which, *Pieces of Africa*, became the biggest-selling classical CD in the USA in 1993. Over 20 dance companies have featured his music, including the White Oak Dance Company, Daniel Ezralow and Judith Marcuse (USA); Shobana Jeyasingh, Jonathan Burrows, Rambert Dance Company and Siobhan Davies Dance Company (London); the Vienna State Opera Ballet (Austria); Roberto Costello (Italy); and Ballet North (Australia).

David Buckland (Designer)

David Buckland is a British-born artist whose scope encompasses photography, portraiture, and set and costume design for the theatre. His career in photography spans almost thirty years. A graduate of the London College of Printing, his first personal exhibition was at Northern Arts, Newcastle in 1972. Since then he has exhibited solo in many international venues: the Sander Gallery (Washington DC), the Musée National d'Art Moderne and the Pompidou Centre (Paris), the Tom Peek Gallery (Amsterdam), and the Museum of Contemporary Photography (Chicago), as well as touring shows in France and Italy. Principal one-man exhibitions include the Photographer's Gallery (London) in 1977 and 1987, the Air Gallery (London) in 1978 and the Éspace Photographique de la Ville de Paris in 1988. An exhibition of his most recent portraits was shown at the National Portrait Gallery in March 1999. Three books of his photographs have been published, including a work on the Trojan Wars featuring the sculpture of Sir Antony Caro. His short film for the 'Dance for the Camera' season, *Dwell Time*, was broadcast on BBC1 in January 1996.

Buckland has designed sets and costumes for over twenty works, primarily for contemporary dance, and many for award-winning companies such as Siobhan Davies Dance Company, Rambert Dance Company and London Contemporary Dance Theatre. He recently created the set design for *A Stranger's Taste*, Siobhan Davies's first work for the Royal Ballet.

Peter Mumford (Lighting Designer, Film Director)

After training in theatre design at the Central School of Art, 1966–69, Peter Mumford became a founder member of the innovative mixed-media performance group Moving Being, with whom he continued to work as a designer until 1978. He has worked widely in dance, theatre and opera throughout Britain and Europe. Over the last six years work has been concentrated on directing (mostly dance and opera) for camera, following the broadcast on Channel 4 of the experimental *Dance-Lines* programme, which he devised, designed and co-produced in 1986. Directing and producing credits include: *The Man Who Strides the Wind* for Almeida Opera (music by Kevin Volans) *White Man Sleeps* and *Wyoming* (choreography Siobhan Davies) for Channel 4; *Heaven Ablaze in His Breast* (choreography Ian Spink) for BBC2; *Dancehouse 1990* for BBC2; *Five Dances by Martha* for La Sept/Cameras Continentale/BBC; *Così Fan Tutte* for Cameras Continentale; *Swan Lake* (choreography Matthew Bourne) for Adventures in Motion Pictures (nominated for an Emmy Award); *Nutcracker Sweeties* for Birmingham Royal Ballet; *Coppélia* and *The Stone Flower* for the BBC/NVC Arts; *Rite Elektrik* and *Carmina Burana* for the BBC; and *Richard II* for the BBC.

Lighting designs for dance include *Fearful Symmetries, Two-Part Invention* (with sets), *Cheating Lying Stealing* and *Mr Worldly Wise* for the Royal Ballet; *The Glass Blew In, Wild Translations, Trespass, Affections, Eighty Eight, Winnsboro Cotton Mill Blues* and *Wild Air* for Siobhan Davies Dance Company; *Carmina Burana, Birthday Offering, Edward II* and *Nutcracker Sweeties* for Birmingham Royal Ballet; *The Sleeping Beauty* for Scottish Ballet; and *Symphony in C* for Munich Ballet. He won an Olivier Award for Outstanding Achievement in Dance in 1995 for his work on *Fearful Symmetries* and *The*

Glass Blew In. He has also worked with the Royal Danish Ballet, Rambert Dance Company, and Second Stride.

Lighting designs for opera include productions for the Royal Opera, English National Opera, Welsh National Opera, Scottish Opera, Opera North, Opera Factory, the Munich Staatsoper and Opera Zuid. Lighting designs for theatre include productions for the Royal Shakespeare Company, the Royal National Theatre, the Almeida Theatre, the West Yorkshire Playhouse, the Royal Court Theatre, the Lyric Hammersmith and Théâtre de Complicité.

Scott Clark (Dancer)

Originally from New Mexico, Scott Clark trained as a dancer after taking a BSc in mathematics, then went on to take an MA in dance from Ohio State University. He is also certified as a movement analyst by the Laban/Bartenieff Institute in New York City. While in New York, he danced for Bebe Miller; after moving to Britain, he was a founder member of Siobhan Davies Dance Company, and received a London Dance and Performance Award for his work with them. He also danced in his own choreography throughout Britain and Europe. He has taught at several American universities, and at most British training centres for contemporary dance. With Suzie Ater, he began the series of daily independent dance classes that now continues at the Jerwood Space, London. He has conducted courses from Finland to Ecuador, and taught for Siobhan Davies Dance Company from its inception until 1997. In 1990, he qualified as a Feldenkrais practitioner, and now devotes his time to that work, specialising in the movement needs of dancers and other performers.

Paul Douglas (Dancer)

Paul Douglas joined London Contemporary Dance Theatre upon graduating from London Contemporary Dance School. He went on to dance with Rambert Dance Company, Reflex Dance Company and the Gregory Nash Group, becoming a founder member of Siobhan Davies Dance Company in 1988. In 1993 he founded Small Bones Dance Company. He teaches extensively throughout the UK and abroad, leading class for major companies and professional schools and studios. Paul has been practising Aikido for 20 years, and is currently the Head Master of Tetsushinkan Budojo at Moving East.

Michael Fulwell (Dancer)

Michael Fulwell began taking classes in contemporary dance at the age of 20, while studying vehicle engineering at Loughborough University. After completing his degree, he took a one-year course at London Contemporary Dance School, staying on for a second year as a founding member of the 4D performance group. Michael was a member of Siobhan Davies Dance Company for its first three years, during which time he also worked with Kim Brandstrup's Arc Dance Company, and with Darshan Singh Bhuller in his dance-for-television project, *The Fall.* He left dance in 1992, joining the Fire Service. He is currently a Sub-Officer in the Royal Berkshire Fire and Rescue Service.

Lauren Potter (Dancer)

Lauren Potter trained at London Contemporary Dance School and subsequently danced with London Contemporary Dance Theatre (LCDT). She left LCDT in 1988 to become a founder member of Siobhan Davies Dance Company. Since becoming a freelance dancer and teacher she has been involved in a wide diversity of dance projects, both staged and televised. She rejoined Siobhan Davies Dance Company in 1998.

Catherine Quinn (Dancer)

Catherine Quinn trained in Australia and performed with Expressions and Dance North. In 1988 she danced briefly with Siobhan Davies Dance Company before joining Rambert Dance Company. Since leaving Rambert, Catherine has worked with Jeremy James, Colin Poole and Small Bones and taught at London Contemporary Dance School. She rejoined Siobhan Davies Dance Company in 1994.

The Degas Quartet (Musicians)

The Degas Quartet, formed in 1988, was set up to work with other artistic disciplines and with composers not normally associated with the string quartet medium. In 1988 the quartet joined forces with Siobhan Davies Dance Company for its premiere of *White Man Sleeps*. In 1990 it was decided to rename the group the Smith Quartet, and since this time the Smith Quartet have established an international reputation for their dynamic and original approach to contemporary music. They have developed a repertoire by some of the world's most exciting composers. Michael Nyman, Sally Beamish, Graham Fitkin and Django Bates, among others, have all written for the quartet. Collaborations include work with Andy Sheppard and John Harle (saxophonists), Thomas Lang and Sarah Leonard (singers), and Siobhan Davies Dance Company, Shobana Jeyasingh and Ultima Vez (dance companies). In 1994 they were awarded a Prudential Award for the Arts.

Production Credits

White Man Sleeps: A Production History

1988   Three-week rehearsal period for original piece. Lizie Saunderson replaced in the final moments by Catherine Quinn.

1988   Premiere of *White Man Sleeps*, Riverside Studios, London. Catherine Quinn performed the role developed by Lizie Saunderson.

1989   Filming of original piece.

1989   Tour of original piece. Gill Clarke replaces Catherine Quinn.

1997   Rehearsal period for revival.

1997   Revival tour.

1988 Production, Riverside Studios

Dancers: Scott Clark
            Paul Douglas
            Michael Fulwell
            Lauren Potter
            Catherine Quinn

Musicians: The Degas Quartet
            Steven Smith (violin)
            Clive Hughes (violin)
            Nic Pendlebury (viola)
            Tanya Smith (cello)

Lighting design: Peter Mumford

Set and costume design: David Buckland

1997 Production, Revival

Dancers: Gill Clarke
            Sean Feldman
            David Hughes
            Paul Old
            Deborah Saxon/Sarah Warsop

Musicians: Carole Cerasi (prepared harpsichord)
            James Johnstone/Vincent Ranger (prepared harpsichord)
            Reiko Ichise (viola da gamba)
            Matteo Fargion (percussion)

Lighting design: Peter Mumford

Set and costume design: David Buckland

Costumes made by: Sasha Keir

Choreography by Siobhan Davies

Date and title, with credits for music, design, lighting, costumes, company and place of premiere.

Abbreviations: M., music; D., design; L., lighting; C., costumes
        LCDT, London Contemporary Dance Theatre
        SDDC, Siobhan Davies Dance Company

1972 Relay

M. Colin Wood, Bernard Watson. L. Michael Alston. LCDT, London.

1974 Pilot

M. Igg Welthy, Stephen Barker. L. Charter. LCDT, Southampton.

The Calm

M. Geoffrey Burgon. L. Charter. LCDT, Manchester.

1975 Diary

M. Gregory Rose. L. Charter. LCDT, Liverpool.

1976 Step at a Time

M. Geoffrey Burgon. L. Charter. LCDT, Manchester.

1977 Nightwatch (*with Micha Bergese, Robert Cohan, Robert North*)

M. Bob Downes. D. Norberto Chiesa. L. Charter. LCDT, London.

Sphinx

M. Barrington Pheloung. L. Charter. LCDT, Manchester.

1978 Then You Can Only Sing

M. Judyth Knight. D. Jenny Henry. L. Charter and Adrian Dightam. LCDT, Manchester.

1979 Celebration

M. 10th and 15th century music arr. Nicholas Carr. D. Caroline Fey. L. John B. Read.
Ballet Rambert, Horsham.

Ley Line

M. Vincent Brown. D. Craig Givens. LCDT, London.

1980 Something to Tell

M. Benjamin Britten. D. Antony Mc- Donald. L. Peter Mumford. LCDT, Mold.

Recall

M. Vincent Brown. L. Peter Mumford LCDT, London.

If My Complaints Could Passions Move

M. Benjamin Britten. London School of Contemporary Dance, London.

1981 Plain Song

M. Erik Satie. D. David Buckland. L. Peter Mumford. Siobhan Davies and Dancers,
London.

Standing Waves

M. Stuart Dempster. D. David Buckland. L. Peter Mumford. Siobhan Davies and Dancers,
London.

Free Setting

M. Michael Finnissy. D. David Buckland. L. Peter Mumford. LCDT, Coventry.

1982 Mazurka Elegiaca

M. Benjamin Britten. Solo for Linda Gibbs, King's Lynn.

Rushes

M. Michael Finnissy. D. David Buckland. L. Peter Mumford. Second Stride, Oxford.

Carnival

M. Camille Saint-Saëns. D. David Buckland, Antony McDonald. L. Peter Mumford. Second Stride, Coventry.

1983 The Dancing Department

M. J.S. Bach. D. David Buckland. L. Peter Mumford. LCDT, Oxford.

Minor Characters

Text, Barbara McLauren. D. Antony McDonald. L. Peter Mumford. Second Stride, Edinburgh.

1984 New Galileo

M. John Adams. D., L. David Buckland, Peter Mumford. LCDT, Leeds.

Silent Partners

M. Orlando Gough. D. David Buckland. L. Peter Mumford. Second Stride, Brighton.

1985 Bridge the Distance

M. Benjamin Britten. D. David Buck- land. L. Peter Mumford. LCDT, Oxford.

The School for Lovers Danced

M. W.A. Mozart. L. Peter Mumford. Second Stride, Hexham.

1986 The Run to Earth

M. Brian Eno. D. David Buckland, Russell Mills. L. Peter Mumford. LCDT, Eastbourne.

and do they do

M. Michael Nyman. D. David Buckland. L. Peter Mumford. LCDT, London.

1987 Red Steps

M. John Adams. D. Hugh O'Donnell. L. Charter. LCDT, Canterbury.

1988 Play within play from Ron Daniels' production of Hamlet

Royal Shakespeare Company, London.

Embarque

M. Steve Reich. D. David Buckland. L. Peter Mumford. Rambert Dance Company, Manchester.

White Man Sleeps

M. Kevin Volans. D. David Buckland. L. Peter Mumford. SDDC, London.

Wyoming

M. John Marc Gowans. D. David Buckland. L. Peter Mumford. SDDC, London.

1989 Sounding

M. Giacinto Scelsi. L. Peter Mumford. Rambert Dance Company, Nottingham.

Cover Him with Grass

M. Kevin Volans. D. David Buckland. L. Peter Mumford. C. David Buckland. SDDC, London.

Drawn Breath

M. Andrew Poppy. D. Hugh O'Donnell. L. Peter Mumford. C. Hugh O'Donnell. SDDC, London.

1990 Signature

M. Kevin Volans. D. Kate Whiteford. L. Peter Mumford. Rambert Dance Company, Brighton.

Dancing Ledge

M. John Adams. D. David Buckland. L. Peter Mumford. English National Ballet, London.

Different Trains

M. Steve Reich. D. David Buckland. L. Peter Mumford. C. David Buckland. SDDC, London.

1991 Arctic Heart

Text, Gretel Ehrlich. M. John Marc Gowans. D. David Buckland. L. Peter Mumford. C. David Buckland. SDDC.

1992 Winnsboro Cotton Mill Blues

M. Frederic Rzewski, with tape by Mark Underwood, Roger Heaton. L. Peter Mumford. C. Sasha Keir. Rambert Dance Company.

White Bird Featherless

M. Gerald Barry. D. David Buckland. L. Peter Mumford. C. Antony McDonald. SDDC, Mold.

Make-Make

Tape compiled by David Buckland. D. David Buckland. L. Peter Mumford. C. David Buckland. SDDC.

1993 Wanting To Tell Stories

M. Kevin Volans. D. David Buckland. L. Peter Mumford. C. Antony McDonald. SDDC, Brighton.

1994 Between the National and the Bristol

M. Gavin Bryars. CandoCo, Nottingham.

The Glass Blew In

M. Gavin Bryars. D. David Buckland. L. Peter Mumford. C. Antony McDonald. SDDC, Bracknell.

1995 Wild Translations

M. Kevin Volans. D. David Buckland. L. Peter Mumford. C. Sasha Keir. SDDC, Sheffield.

The Art of Touch

M. Domenico Scarlatti, Matteo Fargion. D. David Buckland. L. Ian Beswick. C. Sasha Keir. SDDC, Manchester.

1996 Trespass

M. Gerald Barry. D. David Buckland. L. Peter Mumford. C. Sasha Keir. SDDC, Blackpool.

Affections

M. G.F. Handel, arr. Gerald Barry. D. David Buckland. L. Peter Mumford. C. Sasha Keir. SDDC, Oxford.

1997 Bank

M. Matteo Fargion. D. David Buckland. L. Ian Beswick. C. Sasha Keir. SDDC, Blackpool.

1998 Eighty-Eight

M. Conlan Nancarrow. D. David Buckland. L. Peter Mumford. C. Antony McDonald. SDDC, Oxford.

128 | White Man Sleeps: Appendices

1999 Wild Air

M. Kevin Volans. D. David Buckland. L. Peter Mumford. C. Sasha Keir. SDDC, Oxford.

Thirteen Different Keys

M. Marin Marais. D. David Scholefield. L. Peter Mumford. C. Sasha Keir. Artangel commission, London.

A Stranger's Taste

M. 18th-century composers, Marin Marais, Saint Colombe. D. David Buckland. L. Peter Mumford. C. David Buckland, Sasha Keir. The Royal Ballet, London.

Televised Works

1983 Plain Song

Dir. Geoff Dunlop, Channel 4.

Carnival

Dir. Geoff Dunlop, Channel 4.

1985 Silent Partners

Dir. David Hinton, London Weekend Television, South Bank Show.

1986 Bridge the Distance

Dir. Colin Nears, BBC2.

1987 3 untitled pieces in Dance Lines

Dir. Terry Braun, Channel 4.

1989 White Man Sleeps

Dir. Peter Mumford, Channel 4.

Wyoming

Dir. Peter Mumford, Channel 4.

1995 White Bird Featherless

Dir. Peter Mumford, BBC2.

1998 The Art of Touch

Dir. Ross MacGibbon, BBC2.

Siobhan Davies Dance Company

Siobhan Davies Dance Company was founded in 1988. It was set up to create work on an intimate scale and to provide a creative environment for mature dancers to explore and develop their art; and one that could be more fluid and responsive to their needs than was possible in the larger repertory companies.

The Company is committed to making new work and presenting and performing it to the highest standards. The artistic development of Siobhan Davies and the artists with whom she collaborates, such as Kevin Volans, David Buckland, Sasha Keir and Peter Mumford, and the development of the dancers as individual and mature artists, is essential to the Company's unique aesthetic and its working ethos.

Each year the Company premieres new work, revives past works and tours a flexible programme throughout the UK and internationally for 12 to 14 weeks. This touring is supported by a further 20 to 22 weeks of creation, rehearsal and education work.

In addition the Company undertakes special projects, which in 1998 included the BBC filming of *The Art Of Touch*, and in 1999 included working with Artangel and the Royal Ballet to create a site-specific work, *13 Different Keys*, for the Atlantis Gallery in Brick Lane, London.

The Company's work is core funded by the Arts Council of England, and the Company has also attracted significant project funding to support the expansion of its touring, education, audience development and outreach work, following increasing demand from promoters, dance agencies and education establishments.

Siobhan Davies Dance Company is an artist-led organisation and works to ensure that its artistic work is the core point of reference for all its activities. The Company seeks to create an environment which nurtures the individual development of all its members, artistic, managerial and technical.

From its beginnings when the Company was managed from the home of Siobhan Davies, the administrative base has developed into a structure which facilitates and supports the extensive programme of activities undertaken by Siobhan Davies and Siobhan Davies Dance Company.

1999 Organisational Structure

Artistic Director Siobhan Davies MBE
Executive Director Siân Alexander
Associate Director David Buckland
Production Manager Ollie Brown
Marketing Manager Simon Gough
Press Liaison Faith Wilson
Administrator Kirsty Lloyd
Administrative Assistant Sarah Richardson

Artistic Director's Assitant Deborah Saxon
Rehearsal Director Amanda Britton
Board of Directors Peter Barker
　　　　　　　　　Julian Forrester
　　　　　　　　　Katharine Herbert
　　　　　　　　　Marie McCluskey MBE
　　　　　　　　　The Hon. Lady Laura Phillips
　　　　　　　　　Hugo Stewart

Key Sources and Bibliography

Key Sources

Dance Now, Vol. 6, No. 1, Spring 1997.
Special issue on Siobhan Davies.

Dance Theatre Journal, Vol 12., No. 4, Spring 1996.
Special issue on Siobhan Davies.

Jordan, S., *Striding Out: Aspects of Contemporary and New Dance in Britain*, London, Dance Books, 1992.
A chapter and appendix on Siobhan Davies, plus contextual history about the development of contemporary and New Dance.

Jordan, S., and Allen, D. (eds), *Parallel Lines: Media Representations of Dance*, London, John Libbey, 1993.
Many useful chapters on filming dance, including many references to Dance-Lines productions, and a discussion on the filming of *White Man Sleeps* and *Wyoming*.

Sanders, L., *Siobhan Davies: The Development of a Choreographic Style*, Guildford, National Resource Centre for Dance, 1993.

Thrift, J. (ed.), *Siobhan Davies in Residence: Seminar Programme*, Roehampton Institute London, 1996.
Proceedings of the seminars while Davies was choreographer-in-residence at Roehampton Institute London.

Video
Siobhan Davies Dance Company, *White Man Sleeps*, *Wyoming*, Dance Videos, DV15.

Score
Volans, K., String Quartet No. 1: *White Man Sleeps*, London, Chester Music.

CDs
Volans, K., *Cover Him With Grass*, Landor CTLCD111, 1990.
Not currently available, but it does contain both the original version and the string quartet version of *White Man Sleeps*.

Kronos Quartet: *Pieces of Africa*, Nonesuch, 7559-79275-2.
Includes the string quartet version of *White Man Sleeps*.

Bibliography

Alston, R., 'Siobhan Davies: Richard Alston Pays Tribute to a Friend', *Dance Theatre Journal*, Vol. 12, No. 4, Spring 1996, p. 12.

Anon., 'Rigour and Warmth', *Dance and Dancers*, June 1992, pp. 14–15.

Banes, S., *Terpsichore in Sneakers: Post-modern Dance*, Hanover, Wesleyan University Press, 1977.

────── *Democracy's Body: Judson Dance Theatre 1962–64*, Ann Arbor, Michigan, UMI Research Press, 1983.

Bissell, B., 'Siobhan Davies in St Petersburg', *Dance Now*, Vol. 5, No. 1, Spring 1996, pp. 61–5.

Buckland, D. 'Design in Motion', *Dance Theatre Journal*, Vol. 12, No. 4, Spring 1996, pp. 18–20.

Burnside, F., 'Inside the Magic Box', *Dance Theatre Journal*, Vol.7, No. 4, February 1990, pp. 30–1.

────── 'Home Thoughts from Abroad: Distinctive Preoccupations of British Contemporary Dance', *Dance Theatre Journal*, Vol. 9, No. 3, Spring 1992, pp. 30–3, 42.

────── 'Cold Pastoral', *Dance Theatre Journal*, Vol. 10, No. 1, 1993, pp. 44–6.

────── 'Can They Tell Stories?', *Dance Theatre Journal*, Vol. 11, No. 1, 1994, pp. 34–6.

────── 'Television's Summer of Dance', *Dance Theatre Journal*, Vol. 12, No. 2, 1995, pp. 32–4.

Clarke, M., 'London Contemporary Dance Theatre at Sadler's Wells', *Dancing Times*, January 1978, pp. 204–6.

────── 'Siobhan Davies Dance Company', *Dancing Times*, November 1991, pp. 138–9.

Clarke, M., and Crisp, C., *London Contemporary Dance Theatre; The First 21 Years*, London, Dance Books, 1989.

Cohen, N., 'Arctic Heart: Siobhan Davies Dance Company', *Dance and Dancers* 1992, January–February 1992, pp. 27–8.

Cook, C., 'Evolving a Style', *Dance Now*, Vol. 6, No. 1, Spring 1997, pp. 14–19.

Devlin, G., *Stepping Forward: Some Suggestions for the Development of Dance in England during the 1990s*, London: Arts Council, 1989.

Drummond, J., 'Re-arranging the Chairs', *Dance Theatre Journal*, Vol. 12, No. 4, Spring 1996, pp. 6–7.

Early, F., 'Liberation Notes', *New Dance*, April–June 1987, pp. 10–12.

Ensor, M., 'A Novel Approach to Dance', *Sunday Times*, 6 November 1988, p. 7.

Feldenkrais, M., *Awareness Through Movement*, London, Penguin, 1980.

Franks, A., 'Outsider View', *Dance Theatre Journal*, Vol. 12, No. 4, Spring 1996, pp. 8–11.

Gow, G., 'Extremes of Energy: Siobhan Davies', *Dancing Times*, December 1976, pp. 142–3.

Hodgens, P., 'The Choreographic Structure of Robert Cohan's *Stabat Mater* (1975)', in J. Adshead (ed.), *Choreography: Principles and Practice*, Guildford, University of Surrey, 1987.

Hutchinson, A., *Labanotation*, New York, Theatre Arts Books, 1977.

Hutera, D., 'Mind-in-Motion', *Dance Now*, Vol. 8, No. 2, Summer 1999, pp. 63–5.

Jays, D., 'Hervé Robbe, Siobhan Davies Dance Company, Matthew Hawkins and Carlotta Ikeda', *Dancing Times*, December 1995, pp. 271–3.

Jordan, S., 'Second Stride', *Dancing Times*, August 1982, pp. 824–5.

—— 'Rushes (1982): Some Observations', in J. Adshead (ed.), *Choreography: Principles and Practice*, Guildford, University of Surrey, 1987.

—— 'Siobhan Davies: Two for LCDT', *Dance Theatre Journal*, Vol. 5, No. 1, Spring 1987, pp. 12–14.

—— 'Second Stride: The First Six Years', *Dance Theatre Journal*, Vol. 6, No. 3, Winter 1988, pp. 12–14.

—— 'Siobhan Davies Company, 1988', *Dance Theatre Journal*, Vol. 6, No. 4, Spring 1989, pp. 27–8.

—— 'Signs and Designs', *Times Higher Educational Supplement*, 8 June 1990, p. 16.

—— *Striding Out: Aspects of Contemporary and New Dance in Britain*, London, Dance Books, 1992.

—— 'The Collaborations *White Man Sleeps* and *Wyoming*: A Discussion', in S. Jordan and D. Allen (eds), *Parallel Lines: Media Representations of Dance*, London, John Libbey, 1993.

—— *Moving Music: Dialogues with Music in Twentieth-Century Ballet*, London, Dance Books, forthcoming.

Jordan, S., and Allen, D. (eds), *Parallel Lines: Media Representations of Dance*, London, John Libbey, 1993.

Jordan, S., and Thomas, T., 'Dance and Gender: Formalism and Semiotics Reconsidered' in A. Carter (ed.), *The Routledge Dance Studies Reader*, London, Routledge, 1998.

Kane, A. 'Siobhan Davies: Family Connections', Dance Study Supplement, Part 6, *Dancing Times*, Spring 1990, pp. I–VIII.

Kimberley, N., 'Musical Collaborations', *Dance Now*, Vol. 6, No. 1, Spring 1997, pp. 32–6.

Lockyer, B., 'Stage Dance on Television', in S. Jordan and D. Allen (eds), *Parallel Lines: Media Representations of Dance*, London, John Libbey, 1993.

Mackrell, J., 'Stories in Dance', Sadler's Wells programme note, November 1994.

—— *Out of Line: The Story of British New Dance*, London, Dance Books, 1992.

—— 'Siobhan Davies', *Dance Now*, Vol. 6, No. 1, Spring 1997, pp. 4–9.

—— *Reading Dance*, London, Michael Joseph, 1997.

Marigny, C. de, 'Siobhan Davies; LCDT's Resident Choreographer', *Dance Theatre Journal*, Vol. 3, No. 4, 1987, pp. 6–7.

Marigny, C. de, and Newman, B., 'Progressive Programming', in S. Jordan and D. Allen (eds), *Parallel Lines: Media Representations of Dance*, London, John Libbey, 1993.

Mumford, P., 'The Language of Light: Part 1', *Dance* No. 19, Summer 1991, pp. 32–33.

—— 'The Language of Light: Part 2', *Dance* No. 20, Autumn 1991, pp. 29–31.

Novack, C., *Sharing the Dance: Contact Improvisation and American Culture*, Madison, Wisconsin, University of Wisconsin Press, 1990.

Nears, C., 'Bridging a Distance', in S. Jordan and D. Allen (eds), *Parallel Lines: Media Representations of Dance*, London, John Libbey, 1993.

Nugent, A., 'Through a Wide-Angled Lens', *Dance Now*, Vol. 2, No. 4, Winter 1993,